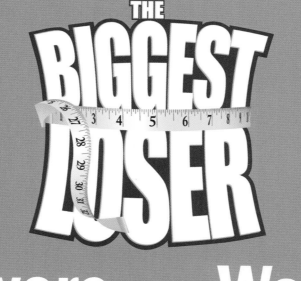

THE BIGGEST LOSER

Flavors of the World

COOKBOOK

THE BIGGEST LOSER

Flavors of the World
COOKBOOK

Take Your Taste Buds on a Global Tour with More Than 75 Easy, Healthy Recipes for Your Favorite Ethnic Dishes

Chef Devin Alexander and *The Biggest Loser* Experts and Cast
with Melissa Roberson

NBC

© 2011 by Universal City Studios Productions LLP. The Biggest Loser is a registered trademark and copyright of NBC Studios, Inc., and Reveille LLC. Licensed by NBC Universal Television Consumer Production Group. All rights reserved. All rights reserved. No part of this publication may be reproduced or transmitted in any form or by any means, electronic or mechanical, including photocopying, recording, or any other information storage and retrieval system, without the written permission of the publisher.

Rodale books may be purchased for business or promotional use or for special sales. For information, please write to: Special Markets Department, Rodale Inc., 733 Third Avenue, New York, NY 10017.

Printed in the United States of America
Rodale Inc. makes every effort to use acid-free ♾, recycled paper ♲.

Book design by Christina Gaugler
Illustration on page 13 by Judy Newhouse
Food photographs by Mitch Mandel and Tom McDonald/Rodale Images
Food styling by Diane Vezza and prop styling by Karen Quatsoe
All other photos by NBC Universal Photo

Library of Congress Cataloging-in-Publication Data is on file with the publisher.
ISBN-10 1–60961–148–9   paperback
ISBN-13 978–1–60961–148–4   paperback

Distributed to the trade by Macmillan
2   4   6   8   10   9   7   5   3   1   paperback

We inspire and enable people to improve their lives and the world around them.
www.rodalebooks.com

Production Development & Direction: Chad Bennett, Dave Broome, Joni Camacho, Steve Coulter, Todd Nelson, Kim Niemi, J. D. Roth, Neysa Siefert, and Ben Silverman

NBCU, Reveille, 25/7 Productions, and 3Ball Productions would like to thank the many people who gave their time and energy to this project: Stephen Andrade, Carole Angelo, Dana Arnett, Sebastian Attie, Nancy N. Bailey, *The Biggest Loser* contestants, Dave Bjerke, Maria Bohe, Jill Bowles, Jen Busch, Jill Carmen, Scot Chastain, Ben Cohen, Jason Cooper, Marie Crousillat, Dan Curran, Dr. Michael Dansinger, Camilla Dhanak, Devin Franchino, Kat Elmore, John Farrell, Cheryl Forberg, Jeff Friedman, Wendy Gable, Christina Gaugler, Marc Graboff, Jenny Groom, Bob Harper, Chris Harris, Robyn Hennessey, Shelli Hill, Dr. Robert Huizenga, Jill Jarosz, Helen Jorda, Adam Kaloustian, Edwin Karapetian, Alex Katz, Allison Kaz, Loretta Kraft, Laura Kuhn, Beth Lamb, Todd Lubin, Roni Lubliner, Alan Lundgren, Carole MacDonal, Rebecca Marks, Jillian Michaels, Gregg Michaelson, John Miller, Sarah Napier, Yelena Nesbit, Jessica Nubel, Julie Nugent, Trae Patton, Ed Prince, Scott Radloff, Lee Rierson, Karen Rinaldi, Melissa Roberson, Beth Roberts, Maria Rodale, Jessica Roth, Drew Rowley, Leslie Schwartz, Carrie Simons, Lee Straus, Kelia Tardiff, Paul Telegdy, Deborah Thomas, Julie True, Josie Ventura, Emily Weber, Liza Whitcraft, Julie Will, Audrey Wood, Yong Yam

Contents

Introduction

Given the fact that I've maintained a 70-pound weight loss for close to 20 years, I truly understand the importance of having options that satisfy all of my (and your!) cravings in a healthy way. And I love that in the 5 years that I've been a part of *The Biggest Loser* family, the producers, executives, trainers, and entire team haven't lost sight of what's truly important: inspiring fans and giving them the tools they need to succeed.

As I was developing the recipes in this book, I joked that I was on the receiving end of some Jillian-style discipline: I was being pushed to a new extreme of creating decadent flavors within some pretty strict nutritional guidelines. When you consider that a typical dish served in an "Americanized" Indian restaurant can have as much as 4,500 milligrams of sodium; that many Asian dishes (even chicken and fish dishes) contain more sugar than my own signature brownies (and probably more sugar than most of the desserts in *The Biggest Loser Dessert Cookbook*); and that Italian dishes can be so full of saturated fat that they're sometimes jokingly referred to as a "heart attack" on a plate, I had quite a challenge to tackle!

In my quest to re-create your favorite ethnic dishes in the healthiest possible ways, I searched far and wide for high-quality, all-natural ingredients that would fit the bill. Admittedly, all of that running around town was sometimes exhausting . . . but it was also fun and eye-opening. Who knew that almond cheese existed and would actually melt perfectly on pizza? And who would have guessed that there are tons of all-natural, salt-free seasoning blends that help create any ethnic dish imaginable, from a Thai seasoning blend to an Indian hot curry blend and even a garlic-herb blend for bread? Just as *The Biggest Loser* contestants are excited to show off what they've learned and gained from Bob and Jillian's workouts at finale time, I'm elated to share what popped out of my oven, off my grill, and even from my stovetop throughout this book.

The next time you have a craving for ethnic food, I hope you'll commit to flipping through these pages before you consider picking up the phone to order takeout. Your mouth is sure to start watering when you see the Sausage & Pepper Goat Cheese Pizza on page 43, Chorizo Nachos on page 115, Crispy Pork Wontons on page 59, and the Tiramisu Custard on page 194. With each bite, you'll see why eating healthy is not only easy, but insanely enjoyable and thus doable for life when you cook for yourself using the right recipes.

I believe that in order to live a healthy life, you have to cook for yourself. Most restaurants just plain don't offer dishes that allow us to indulge without consequence. And as I've worked with contestant after contestant, they always say, "If I could order dishes like these [referring to all of the dishes we've worked on and shared], I'd have no problem making healthy choices!" Well, now they don't have to order them and neither do you.

It's truly an honor to be a part of *The Biggest Loser* community, and I am looking forward to hearing from each and every one of you—from your weight-loss successes, to your cooking challenges and woes, to the types of recipes you want to see in the next book!

Chopsticks, anyone?

Chef Devin Alexander

Notes to the Chef, from the Chef

When I was asked to create healthy makeovers for America's favorite ethnic foods, I admit I was a little nervous. While I've always incorporated plenty of natural ingredients into my recipes, ethnic foods (at least Americanized versions) are typically full of salt, high-fructose corn syrup, and unhealthy fats. While I expected to run into these nutritional obstacles, I had no idea that many of the everyday foods I thought of as "natural" actually included tons of chemicals and preservatives. In my local grocery stores, only one common brand of canned tomato sauce was natural. All other brands contained chemicals. There was no bread whatsoever (not even the "fresh baked" stuff) without additives or sugar. And these are only a couple of examples! I was shocked many times over during the development of this book at the number of foods out there that contained processed sugars and synthetic ingredients.

During my grocery store field trips, I discovered many new (to me, at least) products that are tasty, all-natural substitutes for ingredients I previously used. However, I couldn't find a single all-natural hoisin sauce that tasted good enough for me to recommend, and my team and I tried multiple jars of low-sodium, low-fat, natural marinara sauces before finally finding one that was delicious enough for our recipes. Even though there might not be a natural substitute for every single commercial product out there, I've really done my research and hopefully taken some of the guesswork out of natural grocery shopping for you. I've outlined some of my favorite ingredients for you here, and I encourage you to check out your local natural foods store (or even the natural foods aisle at your grocery store) to acquire these items. Your body will thank you!

Almond mozzarella cheese. I was definitely surprised by how much I enjoyed this naturally low-fat alternative to the cow's milk mozzarella cheese I used to buy. While it doesn't taste like true Italian mozzarella when you eat it on its own, it is really delicious (and even melts like real mozzarella) when used in recipes such as Three Cheese Spinach Lasagna (page 49). I like Lisanatti's almond mozzarella, which is only 50 calories and 1 gram of fat per ounce, making it 97 percent fat free. It also has 7 grams of protein per ounce and only 3 grams of carbohydrates.

Corn tortillas. Most packaged corn tortillas contain tons of ingredients you probably don't want to consume. Make sure to look for tortillas that are 100 percent natural or organic. Just remember, they won't last as long (even refrigerated) as the varieties that contain preservatives, so buy them when you know you need them.

Salt-free seasoning blends. Admittedly, it can be a challenge to create flavorful dishes that are low in fat and sodium. I've always liked using salt-free seasonings to help boost flavor without relying on salt. That said, I wasn't aware of just how many varieties are available. Mrs. Dash has some great new blends that are found at most major grocery stores. I also found some great flavors in the Spice Hunter product line, including Salt Free Cajun Creole Seasoning Blend and Salt Free Fajita Seasoning Blend. Be careful when you buy spice rubs, many of which are salt free but can contain tons of sugar.

Coconut sugar. You may also see it labeled as "palm sugar" or "coconut palm sugar"—that's because it's harvested from the sap of coconut palms. It's completely natural and has a very low glycemic index (it won't spike your blood sugar the way white sugar will), so it's great for all of us health-conscious cooks out there. The flavor is a bit similar to that of brown sugar (not at all like coconut), though not quite as sweet as brown sugar or white sugar. Coconut sugar has a deeper, almost caramel flavor (and color). Admittedly, it can be a bit expensive and hard to find, but it is gaining popularity among consumers (like agave, stevia, and other natural sweeteners), so it's becoming more common. I recommend looking in the bulk bins at your local natural or health food store, or even the natural foods aisle of major grocery chains. (If they don't carry it, it certainly never hurts to ask; you may be surprised that they start stocking it for you). It's also available for purchase online.

Unsweetened plain almond milk. Almond milk is made from ground almonds that are soaked and blended with water, then drained. Unsweetened almond milk has only about 40 calories per cup! Unlike fat-free dairy milk (which has about 90 calories per cup), almond milk is cholesterol free and lactose free. You'll find many commercial almond milks come in plain, vanilla, and chocolate varieties (in this book, I only use plain unsweetened, so be sure to look for that). I've found that not all almond milks are created equal— some brands definitely taste better than others, so if you try one and don't like it, try another brand. Also, note that though it is low-calorie, since it's made from almonds, it does contain some fat (about 3 grams per cup).

Avocado oil. You'll notice that many of my recipes call for extra-virgin olive oil, which I like to use in dishes where you really want the flavor of the oil to come through. But when you need oil for cooking foods over high heat (such as stir-fries), I prefer to use avocado oil, which has the highest smoke point of any natural oil. This oil is rich in monounsaturated fats, which works to lower "bad" (LDL) cholesterol levels. But remember, like any oil, avocado oil is still high in fat (about 14 grams of fat per tablespoon) and calories (120 calories per tablespoon), so always use it in moderation.

Olive oil. The key to using olive oil sparingly is to invest in a mister so that you can spray a small amount on your pans or your finished food as needed. Because many canned olive oil sprays contain propellants and other additives, I suggest that you buy olive oil and then pour it into your mister, which doesn't add any chemicals to your oil but allows you to create a fine spray.

Whole spelt tortillas. Finding an all-natural substitute for commercial whole wheat flour tortillas was quite a challenge. After sampling multiple varieties, I decided on whole spelt tortillas (I like the kind made by Rudi's Organic Bakery; make sure you're buying "whole spelt" and not just "spelt"), because they were the lowest-fat tortillas I could find that were still natural and didn't contain a ton of sodium. If you can afford a little more fat in your diet, there are many other natural, whole grain varieties out there; just make sure to check the sodium content.

Sprouted grain English muffins. I searched high and low for 3½-inch-diameter all-natural, low-fat, whole grain hamburger buns that tasted half as good as traditional hamburger buns. If they exist, I could not find them! A great substitute are Rudi's Organic Bakery Spelt English Muffins or Genesis 1:29 Sprouted Whole Grain and Seed English Muffins. They're a bit higher in calories than what I would prefer to use for a burger or sandwich, but they contain 3 grams of fiber and don't taste "healthy," which is so important to me—I find it's easier to eat healthy when you feel like you're indulging. They're also much softer than many whole grain buns. There are some all-natural hamburger buns available that are pretty good (though I like the Genesis English Muffins over Ezekiel hamburger buns, its sister product, even for hamburgers!), but keep in mind they're probably bigger than the 3½-inch-diameter size I recommend. You can cut the larger ones to size and freeze the scraps for homemade bread crumbs.

Matcha powder. Though I only use this in one recipe, Japanese Tart Green Tea Frozen Yogurt (page 200), it's essential to create the authentic flavor of this Japanese frozen treat. Matcha powder is a finely milled Japanese green tea; make sure to look for unsweetened varieties. "Sweet matcha" contains a lot of added sugar.

Low-fat salad dressings. There are many brands of low-fat dressing available these days, but buyer beware: Low-fat and fat-free salad dressings are commonly filled with chemicals and preservatives (such as monosodium glutamate, or MSG). But you can definitely find brands that are all-natural. A couple of my favorites are Follow Your Heart Low Fat Ranch Dressing and Bolthouse Farms Creamy Yogurt Chunky Blue Cheese Dressing. For a more unique flavor, I love Simply Boulder Culinary Sauces Lemon Pesto. Remember to always check labels for added sugars and be mindful of the sodium content in bottled dressings.

Fat-free evaporated milk. I decided to include this pantry item here because I want to be sure no one mistakes it for sweetened condensed milk, which is very different (both are canned, so they will likely be in the same aisle of your grocery store). Evaporated milk is fresh milk with about 60 percent of the water removed. It contains no added sugar, unlike sweetened condensed milk. Contrary to what you might think, evaporated milk is great for savory as well as sweet recipes. It adds a nice richness to my Steak au Poivre with Cream Sauce (page 178).

Whole grain oat flour. There are many alternatives to white all-purpose flour, but with recipes, it's not as simple as substituting one flour for another. All flours have different levels of starch and gluten, so they bake differently and will lend different textures to the final product. Oat flour is actually oats that have been ground up very finely—in fact, you can even grind old-fashioned oats in your food processor at home and make your own oat flour. It's also available in most major grocery stores (just check the natural foods aisle), your local health food store, and online.

Whole wheat pastry flour. This flour is produced from soft wheat and has a fine texture and high starch content. Because it contains the bran and germ of the wheat kernel, which are removed in white flour processing, it contains more fiber than white flour and is also much denser. I find that on its own, it can have a slightly gritty texture, so I don't recommend swapping it out for white flour unless a recipe gives you instructions for how to do so.

Low-sodium, low-sugar ketchup and barbecue sauce. You'll find many varieties of both of these sauces on the market. It's really a matter of finding ones that taste good to you. Also, note that some ketchups and barbecue sauces might not be marked "low sodium" or "low sugar," so you'll need to read labels and compare to find ones that aren't too high in salt or sugar. If possible, it's better to choose one with a lower-glycemic index sweetener, such as honey or agave nectar, over one that's sweetened with cane juice or sugar.

Creating New Traditions

Each season on *The Biggest Loser*, the contestants come to the Ranch to lose weight and change their lives. In the process, they leave behind their homes, jobs, families, and friends. If there's one thing the *Biggest Losers* have in common, other than a shared commitment to change their lives forever, it's the pride they have in their hometown cultures. They hail from far and wide—the Northeast, the Midwest, the South, the West Coast, and everywhere in between. Over the years, we've even seen contestants whose families originally hail from locations as diverse as Mexico, China, Tonga, and Puerto Rico.

In addition to their devotion to family and heritage, the contestants also have a deep connection to their culture's culinary traditions. At home, they may sit down to a pasta dinner or taco night with their families. But once they arrive at the Ranch, they quickly realize that unless they change their eating

habits, they don't have a chance of changing their lives.

Season 11's Moses Kinikini, whose family hails from Tonga, told the show's medical expert Dr. Robert Huizenga early in the season, "I didn't used to eat until I was full, I would eat until I was *tired*. In the Tongan culture," Moses explained, "about 80 percent of our diet is meat. The rest of it is potatoes and rice. I've learned so much here about nutrition, not only the right things to eat but when to eat it."

Moses says he wants to take what he's learned at the Ranch back to his community to help educate others about the importance of nutrition and fitness. "We're going to go back and show our families," he says. "I know it's impossible to change an entire culture. But I hope to make my community more aware of how food impacts health, because people in my culture often die at a young age. As I watch the younger generation, they're getting very big fast. If we don't change their habits, it's just going to get worse."

Just because the contestants make healthy changes to their diets doesn't mean they have to give up the foods that are central to their culture—and, as you'll see from the recipes in this book, neither do you. Yes, you can lose weight and still eat your lasagna (or burrito or fried chicken), too! It's all about making smart substitutions and revamping recipes to cut back on added fats, sugar, and salt, and incorporating more lean proteins, whole grains, vegetables, and healthy fats into your favorite dishes. Most contestants find that once they start cutting empty carbs, sweets, and processed foods from their diets, they not only lose weight and feel better, but they also actually stop craving the greasy, heavy foods they used to love.

"All the food I've been eating at the Ranch is crazy delicious," says Season 11's Jay Jacobs. "I used to eat a lot of processed foods, but I have taste buds again! The other day, I had steamed asparagus with a little Dijon mustard sauce, and it was so delicious. I never realized how much my senses were dulled by everything I was eating. It's only been a short while, but I'm craving things that I never craved before. And when you work out

Marci Crozier

Planning is the most important part of nutrition. If you shop right, you will have food available at your fingertips to prepare. Lack of planning leads to bad, quick choices because you are so hungry. Planning also helps you keep portions in check. My favorite saying is "Eat to live, don't live to eat!"

this hard, you don't want to put bad things in your body."

Just days into their *Biggest Loser* experience, Season 11's husband-and-wife team JaQuin and Larialmy Allen (who hail from South Carolina) were learning to love and appreciate the taste of steamed vegetables—not something they were used to eating at home. "We didn't eat any vegetables unless they were prepared with sugar, salt, or ham hocks," Larialmy said. ("Or unless they were covered in cheese," added her husband.) "Now I've found myself loving steamed vegetables with no salt, just a sprinkling of black pepper," she continued. "There are also a lot of great spice rubs available that aren't high in sodium. That's a big change for me."

Season 11's Hannah Curlee, who arrived at the Ranch with her sister Olivia Ward, admits that before they came to campus, "We were always exhausted. . . . We were just putting garbage into our bodies. Stepping onto the Ranch, it feels like there's a light in the tunnel for the first time. Putting good things in your body and just feeling your body. . . . It's the best I've felt in years."

Food as Fuel

It's critical for the contestants—many of whom come to the Ranch with a lifetime of emotional pain, setbacks, and other life struggles—to change their outlook on food and see it for what it really is: fuel for the body, not an escape from difficult situations. Many contestants have become so accustomed to turning to food when life gets tough that their emotional eating can be one of their hardest habits to overcome.

Jesse Wornum—whose son and teammate, Arthur, is Season 11's heaviest contestant—knows this struggle all too well, having fought his own battles with drug and alcohol addiction. "I've been clean and sober for 21 years now," he says. "But getting clean was easy compared to the issues I have with my weight. It's one thing to know you have to give up a dangerous substance. But with food, you need it to live. You can't just stop eating. I think that as I begin to understand myself more, I'll be able to conquer the food thing, too."

Arthur Wornum says he also feels the emotional pull of food. "I've had many people ask me, 'Why don't you have gastric bypass surgery?' No offense to anybody who chooses to do that, but I don't think having surgery helps you deal with the issues of why you're eating." Jesse said he devised a strategy at home to help him recognize when he's eating simply for pleasure or distraction. "I put a bell on the refrigerator door so that I could catch myself," he explained. "Most of the time I opened that door, I wasn't hungry. I was bored. I'd be watching the game and a commercial would come on TV. So I'd go to the fridge."

Determined to get to the root causes of their overeating, Arthur and his dad made a pact. "We promised each other that every night before we go to bed, we're going to talk about everything that's on our minds."

Ana Alvarado and her daughter and teammate, Irene, are also familiar with the emotional addiction of out-of-control eating. "I never really had a weight problem until I was pregnant with Irene," says Ana. "Her dad left when I was pregnant. I started to eat out of sadness. I gained weight, and Irene grew up seeing that. I taught her how to be an emotional eater. I feel like I've been responsible for her weight gain."

Working through the reasons why you're tempted to reach for food even when you're not hungry is an important first step in changing the way you look at food. Many contestants also find that once they've made the shift to viewing food as energy for the body, instead of a fun distraction, they want to give their bodies the highest octane fuel they can find. But that doesn't mean they have to give up the flavors they crave. Sometimes it just takes a little creativity in the kitchen.

Sarah Nitta of Season 11 says there's one indulgence she just can't live without: milkshakes. "I really like milkshakes," she said. "The real stuff with the premium cream. But now I make myself a creamy protein shake in the morning, and it actually works well for me. I know it's good for my body. I think about calories in a different way now, as energy instead of fat, and it's such a great thing. I need these calories in my protein shake because I'm going to burn them at the gym. It's a very different mind-set than I used to have."

A Commitment to Change

In addition to making healthy substitutions and creating new versions of their favorite dishes, the contestants have to make a long-term commitment to their new lifestyle and deal with the inevitable temptations and setbacks that come with the journey.

Season 11's Courtney Crozier, whose teammate and mom, Marci, is the manager of a Dairy Queen, says she packs her lunch every day so that

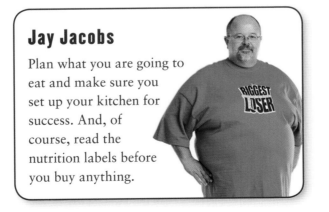

Jay Jacobs

Plan what you are going to eat and make sure you set up your kitchen for success. And, of course, read the nutrition labels before you buy anything.

Olivia Ward

Drink water, water, and more water. Staying hydrated is so important. Water not only hydrates your body, but it also flushes out toxins. Make sure you're drinking enough!

This cookbook celebrates the richness and diversity of local and cultural food traditions. In the pages that follow, Chef Devin Alexander will teach you how to indulge responsibly in your favorite ethnic foods, from Chinese takeout to taco truck fare to the ultimate "ethnic" indulgence: pizza. Whether you grew up in Philadelphia or New Orleans or your family tree extends to Mexico or Italy, you're sure to find recipes that will allow you to celebrate your favorite foods in a healthy way.

she's not tempted to eat unhealthy foods at work. Does she have the occasional bad day? "Yeah," she says. "I do this choice by choice. You screw up one time, you can make a better choice the next time. It's all about a balance in life. That's what I've learned the past year."

Slipups happen. The important thing is to get back to your healthy eating plan as soon as possible after you've wandered from your routine. And if there's a favorite food you just can't live without, figure out how you can eat it in a controlled portion for a special occasion treat. Season 10 winner Patrick House says that while he carefully maintains his calorie budget, "It's unreasonable to think I'll never eat a cheeseburger or a slice of pecan pie again. I will. The difference now is that I won't eat three cheeseburgers or a quarter of a pecan pie."

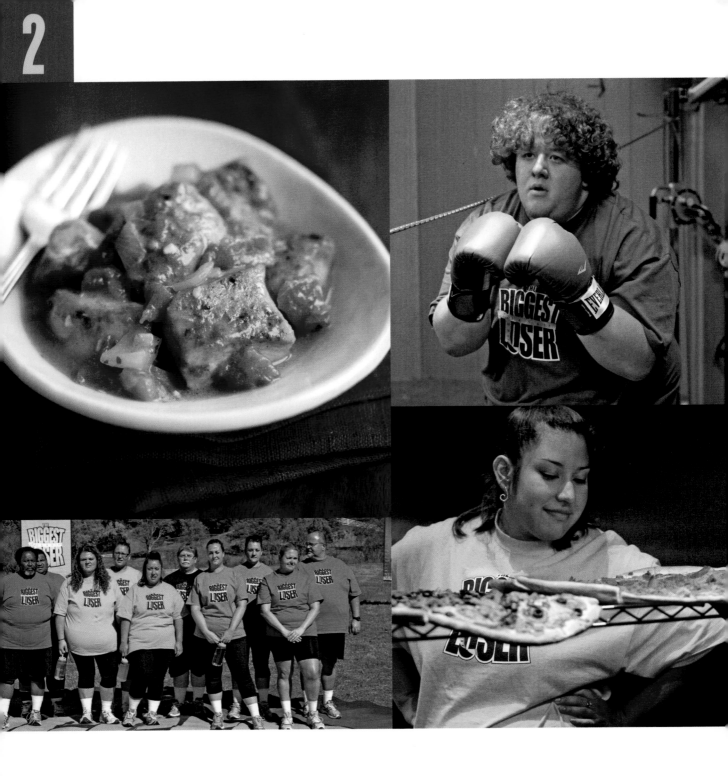

Food as Fuel

Each season on *The Biggest Loser*, the contestants arrive at the Ranch excited to start the process of changing their lives. But many of them are also more than a little nervous about the adjustments they'll have to make to their lifestyle in order to lose weight and get healthy. Not only are the daily workouts with the Biggest Loser trainers long and intense, but the contestants also know that they'll have to change the way they eat—and many of them are reluctant to part ways with the high-fat, high-sugar, high-sodium foods they love.

But they soon discover just how delicious healthy foods can be. They expand their culinary horizons by learning new cooking techniques and how to substitute healthy ingredients for less healthy ones, and by trying foods they've never tasted before.

"Kitchen-allergic" Season 11 contestant Lisa Mosley used to claim that her busy schedule as a single mother didn't leave her with enough time to prepare healthy meals and snacks for her family. Then one day at the Ranch when she needed a little postworkout pick-me-up, she wrapped some turkey breast in lettuce leaves for an instant, protein-rich snack, and it hit her: Time is not the issue. A healthy snack can be thrown together in less than 5 minutes. "Guess I really don't have that excuse anymore," she said.

Elizabeth Ruiz of Season 10 says that the culinary skills and healthy eating tips she learned at the Ranch have helped her to fall in love with cooking. Inspired by the demonstration from guest chef Lorena Garcia, she says she now finds herself cooking for her family more and more. "She really helped me conquer my fear of the kitchen," said Elizabeth. "I grew up in this Hispanic family where the older women ruled the kitchen and I didn't have a place in it. But Lorena helped me see that I do."

Whether you're an experienced cook or a kitchen novice, the important thing is that you first learn about the foods you prepare for yourself and your family, and that starts with understanding the basics of nutrition, calorie counting, and the science of weight loss. In the pages that follow, you'll find the essential tools you need to create a calorie budget and an eating plan that works for you. Once you've mastered your weight-loss plan, it's time to get cooking.

What Is a Calorie?

A calorie is a measurement of how much energy the food you eat provides for your body. You need energy to fuel physical activity as well as all metabolic processes, from maintaining your heartbeat to healing a broken bone or building lean muscle mass. Only four components of the food you eat supply calories: protein and carbohydrates (4 calories per gram), alcohol (7 calories per gram), and fat (9 calories per gram). Vitamins, minerals, fiber, and water do not supply calories.

Keep in mind that the quality of your calories is just as important as the quantity of your calories. Some calories will fuel your workouts, keep you feeling full and satisfied, and help boost your body's immune system and protect you from disease. Other calories (often referred to as "empty calories") don't really provide any benefits—in fact, they can make you feel tired, sluggish, and hungrier than you were before you ate. *The Biggest Loser* plan will show you how to fuel your body the right way. When you give your body the nutrients and energy it needs, you will lose weight and you'll feel better than ever.

The Biggest Loser plan helps you determine the exact daily calorie intake you require to meet your individual weight-loss goals. If you weigh 150 pounds or more, the simple calorie budget formula below, created by *The Biggest Loser* experts, will help you calculate how many calories you need each day. If you weigh less than 150 pounds, talk to your doctor about a calorie budget based on your individual weight-loss needs.

Courtney Crozier

Write everything down that you put in your mouth. Journaling what you eat keeps you accountable. Try not to eat carbs after 7 p.m.; stick to protein and vegetables.

Calorie Budget Calculation:
Your present weight × 7 = Your daily calorie needs for weight loss

As you lose weight, you'll need to continually reassess and reduce your calorie budget in order to keep losing weight and break through plateaus. As you know from watching the show, *The Biggest Loser* contestants lose a lot of weight during their first few weeks at the Ranch. But after they've been at the Ranch for a while and have less weight to lose, they must increase the intensity of their workouts and carefully track their calories to keep losing.

Age is another factor in weight loss. Our muscles burn a lot of calories each day—about 10 times as many as our fat tissue does. But muscles shrink with age, which means we have a natural tendency to burn fewer calories as we get older. But don't use age as an excuse. You should have seen 60-something Estella Hayes of Season 7 flex her muscles at the Season 10 finale in Los Angeles. *The Biggest Loser* medical experts are amazed at how much muscle Estella has added to her body while losing a high percentage of body fat. "Jerry and I are always speaking to groups these days and showing them that age is simply not an excuse," she says about her teammate and husband, Jerry Hayes, who won the $100,000 at-home prize for Season 7.

Allocating Your Calories

Now that you've determined your daily calorie budget, the next step is to figure out how many calories to allocate for each meal and snack. On *The Biggest Loser* plan, you'll eat three meals and two snacks a day.

Divide your total daily calorie budget by four to determine how many calories you should spend on each meal and snack. The example below uses a sample calorie budget of 1,800—yours may be more or less, depending on your goal and starting weight.

Total daily calorie budget: 1,800

$$1,800 \div 4 = 450$$

So for each meal—breakfast, lunch, and dinner—this person has a 450-calorie budget.

Now divide the remaining one-fourth of your total daily calorie budget—in this case, 450—by two.

$$450 \div 2 = 225$$

So, for each of two daily snacks, this person has a 225-calorie budget.

This equation is just a starting point. Use it to help you determine a distribution of calories throughout the day that keeps you satisfied. If you go to the gym in the morning, for example, and require a bigger breakfast to fuel your workout, feel free to shift your calorie intake toward the start of your day. You can move your calorie distribution around to suit your needs and schedule.

If you prefer to eat several small meals throughout the day, you can do that, too. Six 300-calorie meals throughout the day is certainly an option for someone on an 1,800-calorie budget. Many contestants find that eating every 3 or 4 hours is optimal for keeping cravings at bay. Sea-

Don Evans

Remember *why* you are losing weight. Look into the future and imagine how your life and the lives of those around you, especially your family, will be forever changed.

son 10 finalist Alfredo Dinten follows a schedule of eating three meals and two snacks every day. "I'll eat this way for the rest of my life. Why would I change that?" he asked, pointing to his firm abs.

In order to accurately gauge the calorie content of your meals and snacks, you'll need to familiarize yourself with serving sizes. It's important to weigh and measure food so that you know exactly how many calories you're consuming. It's useful to have the following tools (many of which you may already own) to help you measure your portion sizes:

- Liquid measuring cup (2-cup capacity)
- Set of dry measuring cups (includes 1-cup, ½-cup, ⅓-cup, and ¼-cup sizes)
- Measuring spoons (1 tablespoon, 1 teaspoon, ½ teaspoon, and ¼ teaspoon)

- Food scale

- Calculator

Be sure that your food scale measures in grams. (A gram is very small, about $\frac{1}{28}$ of an ounce.) Most of your weight measurements will be in ounces, but certain foods, such as nuts, are very concentrated in calories, so you may need to measure your portion size in grams. There's a wide range of food scales available these days. To purchase the same scale the contestants use at the Ranch, go to www.BiggestLoser.com.

A calculator will be indispensable for tallying your calories at the end of the day. It can also come in handy when the portion size of a food you want to eat differs from the suggested serving listed on its packaging. You may have to do a little math to figure out how many calories you're actually consuming.

When you're making your meals at home, weigh and measure your food *after* cooking. A food's weight can change dramatically when cooked. For example, 4 ounces of boneless skinless chicken breast has around 130 calories when raw. When it's cooked, it'll weigh closer to 3 ounces but will have nearly the same caloric content. The same holds true for vegetables and other cooked foods. Dry cereals or grains, on the other hand, can double or even triple in volume after being cooked with water. Remember that an ounce of weight is not the same as a fluid ounce. You cannot convert the two without knowing the density of the ingredient you are measuring.

After precisely measuring your foods for a week or so, you'll be able to make fairly accurate estimates on your own. Over time, you'll know what right-size portions look like, whether you're cooking a meal in your own kitchen or deciding how much of your entrée to eat in a restaurant (and how much of it to wrap up and take home). But in the beginning, the tools mentioned above can help you get it just right. You can reference the conversion table on page 12 for a list of common measurements and conversions.

Jen Jacobs

Hold yourself accountable for what you are eating by keeping a daily food journal. Even if you eat something unhealthy, write it down! Seeing the sum total of what you put in your body day to day will help you make better choices every opportunity you get.

CONVERSION TABLE FOR MEASURING PORTION SIZES

Teaspoons	Tablespoons	Cups	Pints, quarts, gallons	Fluid ounces	Milliliters
¼ teaspoon					1 ml
½ teaspoon					2 ml
1 teaspoon	⅓ tablespoon				5 ml
3 teaspoons	1 tablespoon	1/16 cup		½ oz	15 ml
6 teaspoons	2 tablespoons	⅛ cup		1 oz	30 ml
12 teaspoons	4 tablespoons	¼ cup		2 oz	60 ml
16 teaspoons	5⅓ tablespoons	⅓ cup		2½ oz	75 ml
24 teaspoons	8 tablespoons	½ cup		4 oz	125 ml
32 teaspoons	10⅔ tablespoons	⅔ cup		5 oz	150 ml
36 teaspoons	12 tablespoons	¾ cup		6 oz	175 ml
48 teaspoons	16 tablespoons	1 cup	½ pint	8 oz	237 ml
		2 cups	1 pint	16 oz	473 ml
		3 cups		24 oz	710 ml
		4 cups	1 quart	32 oz	946 ml
		8 cups	½ gallon	64 oz	
		16 cups	1 gallon	128 oz	

The Biggest Loser Plan

The Biggest Loser nutrition pyramid is made up of fruits and vegetables at its base, protein foods on the second tier, and whole grains on the third tier. The top tier is a 200-calorie budget for healthy fats and "extras."

On *The Biggest Loser* 4-3-2-1 plan, you will eat a daily minimum of four servings of fruits and vegetables; up to three servings of healthy protein; up to two servings of whole grains; and up to one serving of "extras."

45 Percent of Your Daily Calories: Vegetables, Fruits, and Whole Grains

At the base of the pyramid, fruits and vegetables supply most of your daily nutrients in the form of vitamins, minerals, and fiber, and contain relatively low numbers of calories. Aim for a minimum of 4 cups daily of a variety of fruits and nonstarchy vegetables. You can eat more than four servings a day of most fruits and vegetables if you wish, though the majority of your choices should be vegetables.

THE 4-3-2-1 BIGGEST LOSER PYRAMID

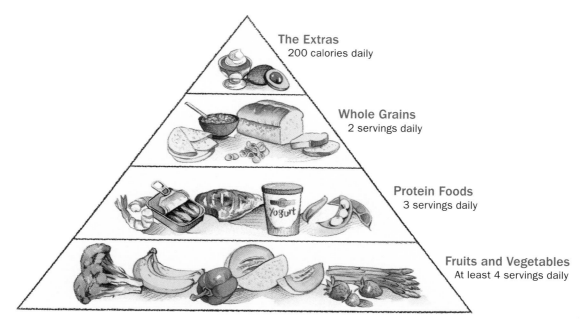

The Extras
200 calories daily

Whole Grains
2 servings daily

Protein Foods
3 servings daily

Fruits and Vegetables
At least 4 servings daily

Vegetables: Serving size = 1 cup or 8 ounces

Tips for eating vegetables:

- When cooking vegetables, avoid added fat. Steam, grill, or stir-fry veggies in a nonstick pan with a spray (not a splash) of healthy oil.

- Try to eat at least one vegetable raw each day. Try a new vegetable each week so that you don't get bored with the same veggies.

- Eat a vegetable salad for lunch or dinner most days of the week.

- Keep precut vegetables such as bell peppers, celery, broccoli, and jicama in your fridge for easy snacking at home or to take to work or school.

- Starchier vegetables such as pumpkin, winter squash, and sweet potatoes are higher in calories and carbs, so limit them to one or two servings per week.

Olivia Ward

Embrace who you are and don't compare yourself to others. Everyone has individual strengths, and as soon as you take pride in those strengths, you will be unstoppable. Love yourself and go for it.

- Fresh vegetables are best, but you can choose frozen, as well. If you opt for canned, be sure to rinse the contents before eating, to wash away added salt.

Fruit: Serving size = 1 cup, 1 medium piece, or 8 ounces

Tips for eating fruit:

- Enjoy at least one whole fruit each day. Apples, oranges, pears, bananas, and grapes are all easily portable and can be eaten for snacks on the go.

- Dark green, light green, orange, purple, red, and yellow: Savor fruits from different color groups. This ensures you're getting a variety of nutrients.

- Eat fruit for dessert! Many *Biggest Losers* who have a sweet tooth use this strategy.

- Opt for fresh fruit over dried fruits, which are more concentrated in calories and sugar and are less filling.

- Choose whole fruit rather than fruit juices. Fruit juice contains less fiber, so it's not as filling as whole fruit, and it's more concentrated in sugars, so it will cause a spike in your blood sugar. When you do choose juice, keep in mind that a serving size is 4 ounces (½ cup).

- Fresh fruit is preferable, but frozen fruit is fine as long as it's not packaged with added sugar or

Irene Alvarado

It's important to watch your salt intake when you're losing weight. The lower the sodium, the better. And don't be shy with the fresh herbs and spices! They taste way better than overly salted food.

syrup. If you choose canned fruit, be sure it's packed in water.

Whole Grains:
Serving size = 1 cup of cooked grains or 2 slices of bread

Choose whole grain foods in moderation, and select those with high fiber content. On *The Biggest Loser* plan, you will eat two servings of whole grains daily. When grains are refined, important nutrients are removed. All that's usually left is starch, which is loaded with carbohydrate calories and little else. Whole grains undergo minimal processing and thus retain most of their nutritional value. The whole grain family includes barley, corn, oats, quinoa, rice, and wheat. These are all great sources of protein, B vitamins, antioxidants, and fiber.

Tips for eating whole grains:

- When choosing bread products, read the label carefully. If it says "enriched," the product probably contains white flour—meaning it's low in fiber and nutrition.

- Choose breads with at least 2 grams of fiber per serving, but aim for 5 grams. When you read the ingredient list, look for "whole wheat" or "whole grain" among the first few ingredients. "Wheat flour" isn't necessarily whole wheat.

- Most packaged breakfast cereals are highly processed and loaded with added sugar. Choose cereals with fewer than 5 grams of sugar and at least 5 grams of fiber per serving.

- White flour, white sugar, white bread, and packaged baked goods affect your blood sugar and insulin too quickly—you don't want an excess of either in your bloodstream. Unlike their whole grain counterparts, these foods also lack antioxidants and fiber. Choose whole grains that will keep you feeling fuller longer.

30 Percent of Your Daily Calories: Protein

Protein is a macronutrient found in meat, fish, eggs, poultry, and dairy products, and in smaller amounts in beans, nuts, and whole grains. Protein is required to build and repair muscle, skin, hair, blood vessels, and other bodily tissues. Generally speaking, any food containing at least 9 grams of protein per serving is a high-protein food.

Lean proteins contain valuable nutrients that can help you achieve a healthy weight. Include protein with each meal and each snack so your body can benefit from it all day long. When you haven't eaten enough protein, you might find yourself running low on energy or suffering from muscle fatigue. Try to eat a little bit of protein or drink a protein shake within 30 minutes after a workout to help your muscles repair. In addition to helping build muscle, protein also promotes the feeling of satiety, or fullness, thus curbing your appetite and keeping you from consuming extra calories. When combined with a carbohydrate (such as a piece of fruit), protein helps slow the release of blood sugar, sustaining your energy for longer periods of time.

Choose a variety of proteins to make up your three daily servings. Try to limit consumption of lean red meat to twice a week, and avoid processed meats, such as bologna, hot dogs, and sausage, which are typically high in sodium and contain nitrates. Fish is an excellent source of protein, omega-3 fatty acids, vitamin E, and selenium.

To figure out how many grams of protein should constitute each of your three daily servings, use the formula below, which uses an 1,800-calorie budget as an example.

1,800 × 0.30 = 540 calories from protein

Then convert the calories to grams.

540 ÷ 4 calories per gram = 135 grams of protein

You can then allocate protein goals for each meal and snack, based on your total daily protein intake. Using the example above, daily protein servings might look like this:

Trainer Tip: Bob Harper

Whatever thoughts you tend to have, your body is going to follow—be it good or bad. When it comes to weight loss, your body can make the transformation. It's your mind you have to work on because it can be the ultimate saboteur. Be aware of negative thoughts and stop playing those old tapes. Focus on the positive things you do each day.

Breakfast: 33 grams

Snack 1: 17 grams

Lunch: 34 grams

Snack 2: 17 grams

Dinner: 34 grams

Animal Protein: Serving size = 1 cup or 8 ounces

Meat

Choose lean cuts of meat, such as pork tenderloin and beef round, chuck, sirloin, or tenderloin. USDA Choice or USDA Select grades of beef usually have lower fat content. Avoid meat that is heavily marbled, and remove any visible fat. Try to find ground meat that is at least 95 percent lean.

Poultry

The leanest poultry is the skinless white meat from the breast of chicken or turkey. When purchasing ground chicken or turkey, ask for the white meat.

Seafood

Seafood is an excellent source of protein, omega-3 fatty acids, vitamin E, and selenium. When you're buying seafood, go for options that are rich in omega-3 fatty acids, such as herring, mackerel, salmon, sardines (water packed), trout, and tuna.

Dairy: Serving size = 1 cup or 8 ounces

Top choices include fat-free (skim) milk, 1 percent (low-fat) milk, buttermilk, plain fat-free or low-fat yogurt, fat-free or low-fat yogurt with fruit (no sugar added), fat-free or low-fat cottage cheese, and fat-free or low-fat ricotta cheese. Light soy milks and soy yogurts are also fine, but if you eat soy because of a dairy intolerance or allergy, be sure to select soy products that are fortified with calcium. Egg whites are another excellent source of fat-free protein.

If you're not eating three servings of dairy per day, *The Biggest Loser* nutrition team recommends that you consider taking a calcium supplement.

Vegetarian Protein: Serving size = 1 cup or 8 ounces

Good sources of vegetarian protein include beans, nuts and seeds, and traditional soy foods, such as tofu and edamame. Many of these foods are also loaded with fiber.

25 Percent of Your Daily Calories: Good Fats

Healthy fats play a role in weight loss because they help you feel full and satisfied. But remember: Even good fats are a concentrated source of calories, and as such, you need to monitor your serving sizes carefully. Many of your fat calories will be hidden in your carbohydrate and protein food choices. You will have a small budget of leftover calories to spend on healthy fat and "extras."

Fats should make up no more than 25 percent of your total daily calories, and saturated fats should account for no more than 10 percent of your daily calorie budget. Here's how to calculate your daily fat intake, again based on the example of an 1,800-calorie budget.

Multiply your total daily calorie budget by 0.25 to see how many calories can come from fat.

$$1,800 \times 0.25 = 450$$

So up to 450 of this person's daily calories may come from fat.

One gram of fat contains 9 calories. So simply divide the number of calories from fat that you're allotted each day (in this case, 450) by nine.

$$450 \div 9 = 50$$

A person with an 1,800-calorie budget would consume no more than 50 grams of fat daily.

Healthy Fats

- Choose olive oil, canola oil, flaxseed oil, or walnut oil for salads, cooking, and baking.

- When adding fat to a sandwich, try using reduced-fat mayonnaise or a little mashed-up avocado.

- Snack on nuts and seeds in moderation. Nut butters, trail mix, and raw nuts pack a powerful energy punch and supply a good dose of unsaturated fat. Keep portion sizes moderate; for example, 14 walnut halves make a 1-ounce serving.

- Choose unsaturated fats. Many unsaturated fats, classified as monounsaturated or polyunsaturated, can lower your LDL (bad) cholesterol and raise your HDL (good) cholesterol.

- Avoid trans fats, an artificial fat found in hard margarines and vegetable shortenings, packaged

Jesse Wornum

Practice consistency: Slow and steady wins the race. Your mental attitude plays a huge role in your physical accomplishments. Build endurance, then strength.

baked goods, and foods fried in hydrogenated fat. Carefully read labels of packaged foods. If you see the words hydrogenated or partially hydrogenated, put the package back on the shelf.

Decoding Food Packaging

Keeping a food journal will require you to become an expert at reading food labels and Nutrition Facts panels. When you're shopping for healthy foods, labels can help you choose between similar products based on calorie and nutrient (such as fat, protein, or fiber) content.

The label on this page is an example of what you'll find on the packaging of any item at your local supermarket. It contains a lot of information, but here is a list of what you most need to evaluate to make healthy choices.

Serving size: Everything else on the label (calories, grams of fat, etc.) is based on this measurement.

Trainer Tip: Jillian Michaels

Saying, "I can't" is not reality—it's a prison that sits in your head. So stop saying what you can't do and instead say what you *can* do because you *can* do anything with the right tools!

Nutrition Facts		
Serving Size		
Servings Per Container		
Amount Per Serving		
Calories 0	Calories from Fat 0	
		% Daily Value*
Total Fat 0g		0%
Saturated Fat 0g		0%
Trans Fat 0g		
Cholesterol 0mg		0%
Sodium 0mg		0%
Total Carbohydrate 0g		0%
Dietary Fiber 0g		0%
Soluble Fiber 0g		0%
Insoluble Fiber 0g		0%
Sugars 0g		
Protein 0g		
Vitamin A 0%	•	Vitamin C 0%
Calcium 0%	•	Iron 0%
Phosphorus 0%	•	Magnesium 0%

* Percent Daily Values are based on a 2,000 calo-rie diet. Your daily values may be higher or lower depending on your calorie needs:

	Calories:	2,000	2,500
Total Fat	Less than	0g	0g
Sat Fat	Less than	0g	0g
Cholesterol	Less than	0mg	0mg
Sodium	Less than	0mg	0mg
Potassium		0mg	0mg
Total Carbohydrate		0g	0g
Dietary Fiber		0g	0g

Calories per gram:
Fat 0 • Carbohydrate 0 • Protein 0

Just because a food label suggests a certain portion doesn't mean that it's the right serving size for you. Look at the calorie and fat content that corresponds to the serving size. If you need to, cut the serving size in half.

Calories: This lists calories per serving. Be sure that the number of calories you record in your food journal reflects the number of calories you've eaten. If the label indicates that a serving is 1 cup and you ate 2 cups, you need to double the calories you record in your journal to match your double serving.

Total fat: The number of fat grams in a product reflects the sum of three kinds of fat: saturated fat, polyunsaturated fat, and monounsaturated fat. Pay special attention to the numbers of calories in "light," reduced-fat, low-fat, and fat-free products. When the fat is removed from many recipes, salt or sugar is sometimes added to enhance the flavor. This can result in a fat-free or low-fat product that actually contains more calories than the regular version.

Saturated fat: Less than one-third of your daily fat grams should come from saturated fats, which are derived mainly from animal products and are solid at room temperature (such as butter and shortening). Some plant oils, such as coconut oil and palm oil, also contain saturated fats. The saturated fat from animal foods is the primary source of cholesterol.

Sodium: For most people, the daily recommended sodium intake is no more than 2,400 milligrams. Some of the foods you eat each day will have more, others less. Aim for an average of no more than 240 milligrams of sodium in each meal or snack.

Total carbohydrate: This number is calculated by adding grams of complex carbohydrates plus grams of fiber plus grams of sugars. If the total carbohydrate number is more than double the amount of sugars, that means there are more "good carbs" than "bad carbs" in the food.

Dietary fiber: Fiber is found in plant foods but not in animal foods. Unless you're on a fiber-restricted diet, aim for at least 25 to 35 grams of fiber per day.

Sugars: The sugars in a food can be naturally occurring or added. Check the ingredient list to find out, and avoid eating foods that contain processed sugars, such as high-fructose corn syrup. The total grams of carbohydrates in a food serving should be more than twice the number of grams of sugar.

Protein: If a food has more than 9 grams of protein per serving, it's considered a high-protein food. It's important to eat foods that are high in protein when you're trying to lose weight, because protein is a great source of energy and helps you feel full.

Ingredient List

A product's ingredients are listed in order of decreasing weight. If the first few ingredients listed include any form of sugar (cane sugar, corn syrup, sucrose, and so on) or fats and oils, the food is probably not a good choice for weight loss. Also, look for products with a short list of ingredients you recognize. A long list of strange-sounding ingredients is always a red flag. Leave those products on the shelf at the grocery store—don't put them on the shelf of your pantry.

Structuring Your Day

As you already know, on *The Biggest Loser* plan, you'll eat three meals (breakfast, lunch, and dinner) and two snacks a day. Parceling out your calories throughout the day means you'll stay full and won't go on sugar or carb binges to satisfy your growling stomach. It also means you won't go to bed feeling stuffed and sick from too many bad, empty calories.

Eating more frequent meals and snacks will:

- Keep you from feeling deprived
- Help control blood sugar and insulin levels (insulin is a fat-forming hormone)
- Lead to lower body fat
- Keep you energized for exercise and activity
- Reduce stress hormones in the body that can contribute to fat accumulation
- Establish a regular pattern of eating that helps prevent impulse eating

Since the contestants are also making a serious commitment to working out, they quickly begin to think of food as fuel. "We work out three times a

Trainer Tip: Brett Hoebel

You are what you eat! Avoid processed foods, as they are usually made with unhealthy chemicals, are harder to digest, and typically have too many calories. Replace them with natural, organic foods that have been on the earth since the beginning, like fresh fruit, green leafy veggies, lean meats, and raw nuts and seeds.

day with our trainers," said Season 11's Justin Pope, a former athlete. "Recently, I started feeling that edge that I hadn't felt since I played sports. It's when you push yourself so hard that there's nothing left to give. You're done. That's when food becomes your friend. You have to eat to have energy again. It's not about starvation, it's about learning what kind of food your body needs so you can have the energy to burn those calories."

Contestants are often surprised to learn that their past habit of skipping meals contributed to their weight gain. The problem with skipping meals is that by the time mealtime rolls around, you're famished and more likely to choose the wrong foods, especially those high in fat. Fat has more than twice as many calories as protein and carbohydrate. It satisfies hunger very quickly, and your body seems to know this. So the longer you go without food, the more likely you are to crave a high-fat treat.

Deni Hill

At the Ranch, I learned that I don't have to be perfect. I just need to try my best and trust my instincts. I can do far more than I ever thought I could!

Sione Fa of Season 7 says he used to skip meals during the day and would be famished by dinner. On the way home, he'd grab some fast-food burgers and polish them off *before* eating his wife's home-cooked dinner. That would be followed by a steady pace of snacking up until bedtime.

The other problem with skipping meals is that when you wait too long to eat, you lose sight of your body's natural hunger cues. You don't really know when you're hungry anymore (or when you're full). Most overeaters don't stop eating when they're full—they stop when they're stuffed!

From starving to stuffed, the hunger scale on the opposite page defines your body's hunger signals and how to interpret them.

If you're not in the habit of eating regular meals and snacks, creating a food schedule that you use in conjunction with your journal can help you stay on track. Successful *Biggest Losers* learn over time that carefully planning their meals and snacks is one of the most important components of successful weight loss.

Planning Regular Meals and Snacks

If you polled *The Biggest Loser* contestants about what they believe is the key to successful weight loss, you'd likely hear the same word over and over again: plan. Planning is essential to

The Biggest Loser Hunger Scale

1. **Famished or starving:** You feel weak and/or lightheaded. This is a big no-no.

2. **Very hungry:** You can't think of anything else but eating. You're cranky and irritable and can't concentrate.

3. **Hungry:** Your stomach's growling and feels empty.

4. **A little bit hungry:** You're just starting to think about your next meal.

5. **Satisfied:** You're comfortable, not really thinking about food. You feel alert and have a good energy level.

6. **Fully satisfied:** You've had enough to eat, maybe a little too much. Maybe you took a few extra bites for taste only, not hunger.

7. **Very full:** Now you need to unzip your jeans. You're uncomfortable, bloated, tired. Maybe you don't feel great. Where's the couch . . . ? You should never feel like this after a meal.

HUNGER SCALE FLASH CARD

1–3: Eat! Eat!

5: Stop, especially if you're trying to lose weight.

6: Definitely stop.

7: You may have waited too long. Better go find the couch and start over tomorrow.

If your hunger is anywhere from level 1 through 3, you should eat.

If you're at level 4, drink a glass of water, chew a piece of sugar-free gum, or do something else to distract yourself from thinking about food.

When you're trying to lose weight, you should try to stop eating when you reach level 5, but definitely no later than level 6. If you get to level 7, you've eaten too much. Anything above that is way too much and will sabotage your weight-loss efforts.

weight loss, and the contestants quickly learn that it's also essential for them to stay competitive and keep their spot on the Ranch. On days when they're going to compete in a physical challenge—which often takes place hours away from campus—they have to plan ahead and pack healthy meals and snacks so they have the fuel they need to perform at their best. Season 5 winner Ali Vincent says she even strategically planned her sleep around these road trips. She used those hours in the van to sneak in catnaps, giving her the advantage of extra energy for some more gym time when they returned home to the Ranch. "I wanted to make every second count," she says.

Breakfast

When it comes to breakfast, rule number one is: Eat it every day, no skipping. If you're not used to eating something within an hour of waking, you'll have to teach your body to re-cue its hunger sig-

nals. Try starting small and eating something simple, such as a bowl of fruit or a slice of whole grain toast with some almond butter. Try to include fiber and protein in your breakfast, which will keep you feeling full all morning.

Lunch

It's easy to eat fast food in the car, buy lunch from a vending machine, or grab a handful of something from the fridge. But you'll probably make better food choices—and enjoy your meal more— if you do a little prep work ahead of time and use lunch as an opportunity to recharge for the second half of your day. As trainer Jillian Michaels points out, fueling your body with healthy food in the middle of the day will keep your metabolism on an even keel.

Make sure your lunch includes a combination of lean protein, complex carbs, and healthy fats. You might have a salad with lots of vegetables and a serving of lean protein, or a sandwich

Trainer Tip: Cara Castronuova

When you dine out, ask how your food has been prepared. If a calorie or ingredient list is available, be sure to read it. You never know how many hidden calories are in prepared restaurant dishes.

Moses Kinikini

For a great, satisfying snack, try a piece of fruit with a little bit of protein, like natural peanut butter or a handful of almonds. And be sure to eat plenty of fiber to keep you feeling full.

made with whole grain bread. You've got a lot to accomplish in your afternoon, so feed yourself wisely!

Snacks

Snacks should be eaten mid-morning and mid-afternoon, a few hours after you've eaten breakfast or lunch, when you're beginning to feel your energy wane. Try to eat something about every 3 to 4 hours, which will help keep cravings at bay, blood sugar stable, and your energy up. Aim for a snack that combines one serving of carbohydrates (such as a piece of whole fruit) with a half serving of protein (such as a low-fat cheese stick). Protein will help you feel full and satisfied, and when combined with carbs, a snack will help keep your blood sugar stable.

When you're away from home, be sure to plan and pack your snacks for the day. Many *Biggest Losers* also find it helpful to keep preportioned snacks in the fridge in plastic bags or reusable containers. They're handy for preworkout pick-me-ups and postgym refueling.

Dinner

Take the time to slow down and enjoy your dinner. Write your shopping list on the weekend and make a supermarket run to ensure you have everything you need for the week in your kitchen. Try to cook a few healthy meals on the weekend that you can refrigerate or freeze in individual portions and heat up as needed for a quick weeknight meal. Plan your weekly menu based on your calorie budget and weight-loss goals.

Dinner doesn't have to be a big, heavy meal. Trainer Bob Harper advises contestants to eat "lean and green" at night, avoiding carbohydrates. For most of the contestants at the Ranch, dinner preparation becomes fairly simple. They might throw together a simple salad of fresh vegetables, grill a chicken breast, or heat up some soup. Their evening meal is no longer the large, three-course food fest many of them had become accustomed to.

Liquid Calories

Your beverage of choice should always be water. If you're not already doing so, make sure to drink eight 8-ounce glasses of water a day to stay properly hydrated. This is especially important when you're changing your food habits and incorporating more fiber into your diet. Record your water intake in your journal each day to be sure you've met your quota.

Staying hydrated improves all bodily functions at the cellular level and helps your heart and kidneys work more efficiently. In addition, water carries glucose, nutrients, and dietary antioxidants to our tissues, resulting in an energy boost and other health benefits. And water actually helps regulate body temperature (especially important for people with poor circulation) and helps you feel full. In fact, some studies have shown that drinking a large glass of water 30 minutes before a meal can help reduce calorie intake during the meal.

In addition to water, coffee, tea, low-fat or skim milk, and protein shakes are other acceptable beverages on *The Biggest Loser* plan. Try to limit caffeine consumption to a minimum, however, and if you're drinking coffee or tea, it should never include syrup, whipped cream, or chocolate! Choose low-calorie beverages such as unsweetened green tea and record them in your journal.

Get Moving

As you know by now, weight loss is all about calories in and calories out. Calculating a calorie budget, planning your meals and snacks, and tracking what you eat in a food journal are all great ways to make sure you are taking in the right number and right kind of calories. But what about the "calories out" part of the equation?

The contestants at the Ranch put in long,

Trainer Tip: Bob Harper

If your family can't give you the love and support that you need, maybe you have to look for that elsewhere. Our family is our family. They're going to do the best they can, but maybe that's not the best for you. You can choose your friends and support system. It's important to tell people what you need. We all have our scars in life; how you can heal them and move forward is the important thing.

hard workouts every day. But you don't have to work out for hours with Bob and Jillian to see results. If you're not already active, start incorporating more activity into your day. Walk or bike instead of driving; take the stairs instead of the elevator; treat your dog to an extra-long walk. It doesn't matter how small you start—you just have to get moving.

If you already exercise moderately, consider increasing the duration (amount of time you exercise) and the intensity (how hard you exercise) to see more results. If you typically walk or run on a treadmill for 30 minutes, try adding an incline, holding some hand weights, or increasing your time by 10 minutes. If you take a beginner's yoga class once a week, ask yourself if you're ready to move to the intermediate level, or take the class twice a week. The more you put into your fitness regimen, the more you will get out of it.

Here are some tools to help you get moving, no matter what your fitness level is today:

Make a Plan

Studies show that people who plan ahead for their workouts are generally more successful than those who wing it. Decide when you want to work out and put it in your day planner. Log that time as yours. After you've exercised, record your accomplishments in this journal.

Kaylee Kinikini

Make your calories count! Instead of choosing high-fat, high-calorie foods, pick healthy foods that still satisfy but contain fewer calories. You can eat more of them and still stay within your calorie budget.

- Set an alarm as a reminder to work out. Or schedule a reminder on your computer, if that's where you spend most of your day.

- Pack your gym bag the night before so that you can grab it and go in the morning.

Build a Team

At the Ranch, contestants are divided into teams to provide support and guidance for one another. You'll need that encouragement, too!

- Plan walking activities with your kids, or encourage a friend to become an exercise buddy.

- Look for workout partners online through sites like www.biggestloserclub.com or through your local colleges, churches, and community centers.

Be Consistent

Experts suggest that it takes 21 days of consistent behavior to form a habit—so don't get discouraged after only a couple of days. Find small ways to stay active, and before you know it, your body will start to crave exercise.

Get FITTE

FITTE is a quick, handy acronym to help you remember all the elements of an exercise routine you need to improve your fitness. It's a good way, especially for beginners, to start thinking about working out. As you begin to make exercise a part of your lifestyle, you'll want to vary or increase some or all elements of the FITTE principle:

Frequency: How often you workout

Intensity: How hard you work out (measuring with a heart rate monitor or using rate of perceived exertion)

Time: The duration of your workout

Type: The kind of exercise you're doing

Enjoyment: How much pleasure you get out of the activity

Frequency

The American Council on Exercise recommends 20 to 30 minutes of cardiovascular exercise 3 to 5 days a week (depending on intensity; a shorter workout duration calls for more intensity) and strength training at least twice a week. You can combine cardio and strength on some days or keep them separate.

Intensity: Load, Speed, and Effort

There are many ways to increase or decrease intensity.

Trainer Tip: Jillian Michaels

Not all fats are the same. Saturated fats and trans fat found in animal products and processed foods increase your chances of heart disease and stroke, so choose healthy fats instead. Cook with canola oil, instead of butter. Substitute that prime rib with salmon. Or swap out your mayo for avocado slices on your sandwich.

- **Load:** This is the amount of resistance you use in your workout. For strength training, you can use your own body weight as resistance or increase the load (and intensity) by adding weights.

- **Speed:** During your cardio workouts, you can amp up intensity by simply going faster. It will help you burn more calories and strengthen your heart. You can vary speed in the strength exercises, too. When exercising with dumbbells, keep your speed under control to ensure that you never swing the weights.

- **Effort:** This is one of the most common ways to vary intensity. There are two ways to measure intensity. The most common is called rate of perceived exertion (RPE), shown on this page, and it is an easy-to-follow self-measurement. Use the rating scale to gauge how your body feels when you're working out. RPE ranges from 6 (no exertion at all) to 20 (maximal exertion).

Calculating Your Target Heart Rate

The rate of perceived exertion scale relates to your exercise heart rate as well. We all have a resting heart rate (our pulse rate when we are immobile), a maximum heart rate (the highest rate we should reach in a workout), and a target heart rate zone (for maximum fat burning). Your target heart

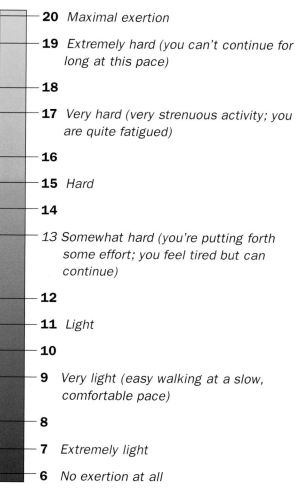

RATE OF PERCEIVED EXERTION SCALE

20 *Maximal exertion*

19 *Extremely hard (you can't continue for long at this pace)*

18

17 *Very hard (very strenuous activity; you are quite fatigued)*

16

15 *Hard*

14

13 *Somewhat hard (you're putting forth some effort; you feel tired but can continue)*

12

11 *Light*

10

9 *Very light (easy walking at a slow, comfortable pace)*

8

7 *Extremely light*

6 *No exertion at all*

rate—the rate that you should aim to achieve in your workouts—can be easily calculated, once you know your maximum heart rate. To find your maximum heart rate, follow this simple formula:

220—your age = Maximum heart rate

So, for a 35-year-old, the maximum heart rate is 185 (220—35 = 185).

Now, to find your target heart rate zone, you're going to use the number you just calculated for your maximum heart rate:

Low-range target heart rate = Maximum heart rate x 0.80

High-range target heart rate = Maximum heart rate x 0.85

So, for the same 35-year-old . . .

- The target heart rate (low range) would be 148 (185 × 80% = 148).
- The target heart rate (high range) would be 157 (185 × 85% = 157).

Marci Crozier

This is hard to say, but it's important to think about *yourself*. Remember, you can be so much more to others if you are energized and healthy yourself first and foremost.

This person should aim to keep their heart rate between 148 and 157 when exercising.

Studies have shown a correlation between rate of perceived exertion and heart rate, with heart rate equaling about 10 times the RPE you've reached. For example, if you're working out at an 11 on the scale, your heart rate should be approximately 110. For the 35-year-old, this would not be in the target heart rate zone. He or she would need to increase the intensity and be more in the 14-to-16 range to achieve the 148-to-157 target heart rate zone. Looking at the RPE scale, this makes sense, as that range represents "somewhat hard" to "hard."

Time

Time (or duration) is how long you actually exercise. We're all challenged to find time to exercise, but it's important to stick to your exercise schedule and put in as many minutes or hours as you can dedicate if you want to achieve your weight-loss goals.

Type

The type of exercise you choose will have a great impact on whether you can maintain a fitness program. If you prefer, fulfill your 30 minutes of aerobic exercise with cycling rather than walking. Studies show that you'll be more likely to stick to an exercise program if you like what you're doing. Other options are swimming, jumping rope, and aerobics classes. If you don't enjoy lifting dumbbells, try using tubing, elastic bands, medicine balls, weighted water balls, and stability balls (go to www.biggestloser.com for products).

Jen Jacobs

Music, music, music! Incorporating music into your workout will help you to constantly push yourself, and it makes the time fly by!

Enjoyment

Ana Alvarado of Season 11 says that after losing her first 50 pounds, she went to a salsa class and fell in love with the fast-paced Cuban dance style. "I love to get out there and move," she said. "And who knows," the single mom smiles, "I might just meet someone!"

You'll find former *Biggest Loser* contestants training for marathons, competing in triathalons, taking yoga classes, skiing, and doing just about any form of physical activity you can imagine. Once you find a form of exercise you love, you're more likely to stick with it and stay dedicated to your workout schedule. And sometimes, physical activity can be as simple as playing with your kids or taking your dog for a walk. The important thing is to just get moving!

3

Italian Reinvented

Recently on the BiggestLoserClub.com message board, a *Biggest Loser* Club member asked who cooks all of the meals for the contestants at the Ranch. The answer? No one! The contestants have access to a beautiful kitchen and a well-stocked pantry, but they must cook for themselves every day. And if they don't know how to fend for themselves in the kitchen, they either make friends with another contestant who knows how to cook, or they learn—fast.

Maria Ventrella of Season 9, whose son Michael won the grand prize, quickly made herself at home in the Ranch kitchen and reinvented her traditional Italian recipes to make healthy versions of her son's favorite dishes. One of her biggest hits? Turkey meatballs made with oatmeal instead of bread crumbs. "Everyone fought over them in *The Biggest Loser* kitchen," she says.

Having grown up with Italian grandparents on both sides of her family, Chef Devin takes her Italian food seriously as well. "One of our staple dinners was spaghetti and meatballs," she remembers. "And we wore our special 'spaghetti shirts' to catch all the sauce." Spaghetti is still one of Devin's favorites, though these days she makes a much healthier version. In fact, when she was testing a spaghetti sauce recipe for this book, she says she loved the results so much that she was "bummed" when one of her containers of sauce fell off the counter and onto the floor—she was hoping to have some later for dinner!

If you have a special spaghetti shirt, now's the time to put it on. Chef Devin has reinvented Italian recipes here so you can indulge without fear. After all, who doesn't love Italian food?

Buon appetito!

CAESAR CHOP SALAD

I think few people realize how fattening a typical Caesar salad is. Sometimes it seems like the only "healthy" option on a restaurant menu, yet in most cases, it's far from being the leanest. In fact, some varieties can contain as many calories as a hamburger! So much for "just having a salad."

5 cups loosely packed shredded romaine lettuce

½ ounce all-natural, low-fat, whole grain pita chips or croutons, broken into crouton-size pieces (I used Whole Foods 365 Everyday Value Whole Wheat Pita Chips with Flax & Onion)

½ ounce all-natural shaved Parmesan cheese

2 tablespoons all-natural, low-fat creamy yogurt Caesar dressing (I used Bolthouse Farms Creamy Yogurt Caesar Parmigiano Dressing)

4 ounces sliced Essential Grilled Chicken (page 205)

Ground black pepper (optional)

Place the lettuce, croutons, and half of the cheese in a medium glass or plastic mixing bowl. Drizzle with the dressing and toss well to coat. Transfer it to a serving plate and place the sliced chicken on top. Sprinkle the remaining cheese over top. Season with pepper, if desired. Serve immediately.

Makes 1 serving

Per serving: **330 calories, 35 g protein, 20 g carbohydrates (4 g sugar), 12 g fat, 4 g saturated fat, 83 mg cholesterol, 6 g fiber, 452 mg sodium**

Trainer Tip: Cara Castronuova

As a delicious and calorie-free substitute for salad dressing, try squeezing some fresh lemon juice onto your salad and sprinkle it lightly with a little salt and pepper.

ORZO ANTIPASTO SALAD

If you've never roasted your own red bell peppers, it's a simple process and will save you from the sodium that's contained in most jarred varieties (about 250 milligrams in a ½ cup-serving). Simply poke the peppers with a knife once on each of the four sides. Place the peppers on a grill or under a broiler until the skin on one side is blackened. Rotate the pepper one-quarter turn, and grill or broil until the skin on that side is blackened. Continue until the skin on all sides is blackened, then transfer the pepper to a paper bag. Close the bag and let the pepper cool for 10 to 15 minutes. Remove the pepper. The skin should easily peel off. Remove the core and seeds, and you now have the freshest, leanest roasted peppers ever!

6 ounces dry whole wheat orzo pasta (about 1 scant cup)

3 ounces nitrate-free turkey salami, cut into ¼" strips

3 ounces nitrate-free turkey ham steak, cut into ¼" cubes

1½ cups chopped fresh spinach

1 cup seeded and chopped tomatoes

½ cup roasted red bell pepper strips (homemade, not soaking in brine or containing preservatives)

⅓ cup zucchini matchsticks

2 tablespoons drained canned sliced black olives

2 tablespoons fresh basil slivers, or more to taste

2 tablespoons red wine vinegar, or more to taste

2 tablespoons freshly grated all-natural Parmesan or Romano cheese

2 teaspoons freshly minced garlic

½ tablespoon extra-virgin olive oil

Ground black pepper

Crushed red pepper flakes, to taste (optional)

Cook the orzo according to package directions, omitting any butter or oil. When cooked, transfer it to a strainer and run it under cold water. Drain well.

In a medium mixing bowl, combine the orzo, salami, ham, spinach, tomatoes, bell pepper, zucchini, olives, and basil. Mix until well combined. Add the vinegar, cheese, garlic, and oil and mix. Season with black pepper and pepper flakes, if desired. Serve immediately or refrigerate for up to 3 days.

Makes 4 (1¾-cup) servings

Per serving: 260 calories, 14 g protein, 38 g carbohydrates (4 g sugar), 6 g fat, 1 g saturated fat, 31 mg cholesterol, 6 g fiber, 407 mg sodium

CAPRESE BOWL

This beautiful and delicious take on the traditional caprese salad contains all of the colors of the Italian flag. Try serving it in a martini glass or decorative bowl as an elegant start to a dinner party.

1 cup halved grape or pearl tomatoes

1 ounce almond mozzarella cheese (I use Lisanatti), cut into ½" cubes

5 medium basil leaves, cut into thin slivers, or more to taste

½ teaspoon extra-virgin olive oil

½ tablespoon balsamic vinegar, or more to taste

Sea salt, to taste

Ground black pepper, to taste

Add the tomatoes, cheese, basil, oil, and vinegar to a medium resealable plastic container. Toss until well combined and season with salt and pepper. Refrigerate for 30 minutes, then serve.

Makes 1 serving

Per serving: **103 calories, 8 g protein, 10 g carbohydrates (5 g sugar), 4 g fat, trace saturated fat, 0 mg cholesterol, 3 g fiber, 200 mg sodium**

Trainer Tip: Bob Harper

You may step on the scale sometimes, and it won't make you happy. But remember all the good you're doing for yourself. Keep the big picture in mind. You're getting your life and health back. It's really important to celebrate those victories. You can't let that number define you.

PROSCIUTTO-WRAPPED MELON

Most restaurants serve this dish drizzled with plenty of extra-virgin olive oil. Plus, the prosciutto often contains nitrates. I much prefer this extremely simple, yet elegant version that is also a bit easier on my (and your) heart and hips.

Note that most packaged prosciutto is sliced extremely thinly, which is how it should be for this recipe. If you are buying it from the deli counter, be sure to request that it is sliced as thinly as possible.

---

4 (5½" long by 1¼" wide) strips (about ½ ounce total) trimmed, all-natural prosciutto (with no more than 3.5 grams of fat per ounce)

4 (1½") cubes honeydew or cantaloupe, or a combination

Olive oil spray (propellant free)

Ground black pepper, to taste (optional)

Wrap a strip of prosciutto evenly around one of the cubes of melon so that the ends join at the top. Poke a decorative toothpick standing upright into the center to secure it. Repeat with the remaining prosciutto and melon. Lightly mist the cubes with spray. Season with pepper, if desired. Serve immediately.

Makes 1 serving

Per serving: 90 calories, 6 g protein, 12 g carbohydrates (10 g sugar), 2 g fat, <1 g saturated fat, 6 mg cholesterol, 1 g fiber, 365 mg sodium

Alfredo Dinten, Season 10

You have to watch the olive oil when it comes to Italian cooking. I've started just using a spritz of canola or olive oil when I sauté onions and garlic for tomato sauce, instead of pouring olive oil into a pan. It still tastes great!

PROSCIUTTO RICOTTA BRUSCHETTA WITH CARAMELIZED ONIONS

Though prosciutto is generally served with visible fat remaining, I always trim the fat from it—it's just not worth all of the empty, bad-fat calories. You'll also get a stronger flavor of the actual meat that way.

When you first open your container of ricotta, pour off any excess liquid. My favorite brands don't have any liquid at the top, but many others do. If you stir the liquid into the container, your finished dish won't be as rich in taste.

Olive oil spray (propellant free)

1 cup thinly sliced red onion

½ teaspoon coconut sugar

Sea salt, to taste

Ground black pepper, to taste

2 (2-ounce) pieces all-natural whole wheat or whole grain baguette (see note)

½ cup all-natural fat-free ricotta cheese, drained of any liquid on top of the container

½ ounce all-natural prosciutto, trimmed (with no more than 3.5 grams of fat per ounce) and sliced into thin strips

1 teaspoon balsamic vinegar, or more to taste

1 tablespoon fresh basil slivers

Place a small nonstick skillet over medium heat. When hot, mist it with spray and add the onion and sugar. Season with salt and pepper. Cook, stirring occasionally, for 5 to 7 minutes, or until the onions are tender and caramelized.

Meanwhile, toast the baguette pieces. While they are still warm, spread ¼ cup of the ricotta evenly over each piece. Top each evenly with half of the prosciutto, then half of the onions. Drizzle each bruschetta piece with ½ teaspoon of the vinegar and top each evenly with the basil. Serve immediately.

Makes 2 servings

Note: *Depending on the exact shape and size of your baguette, the 2-ounce piece you use in this recipe will vary in length, though I find that a piece about 6" long is usually around 2 ounces.*

Per serving: 219 calories, 14 g protein, 34 g carbohydrates (6 g sugar), 2 g fat, trace saturated fat, 3 mg cholesterol, 3 g fiber, 405 mg sodium

Hannah Curlee

Get a workout buddy. Keep moving! The more you move, the more calories you burn. If you're not able to hit the gym, recruit a friend to walk with you in your neighborhood.

SAUSAGE & PEPPER GOAT CHEESE PIZZA

If you have a pizza stone and pizza peel, I highly recommend you use them to make this pizza. This will give it a pizza-parlor-quality taste, which can't quite be achieved by cooking it in a pan, though it's still delicious when cooked that way, too.

Note that you should not spray your nonstick pizza pan with cooking oil or add any fat to it. If you do, it will be impossible to press the dough out. The grease will make it shrink back toward the center of the pan. Also note that the sausage in this recipe should not be eaten on its own. Though it tastes great as part of this pizza—given the saltiness of the dough, cheese, and sauce—on its own, it requires the addition of salt to give it the flavor of traditional sausage.

---

12 ounces extra-lean ground turkey (I use Jennie-O)

2 teaspoons fennel seeds

2 teaspoons dried parsley

½ teaspoon crushed red pepper flakes, plus more to taste

1 teaspoon Italian seasoning

½ teaspoon garlic powder

Olive oil spray (propellant free)

1 cup thin, 1½"-long green bell pepper strips

16 ounces all-natural, low-fat whole wheat pizza dough (see note on page 44)

1 cup all-natural low-fat, low-salt, no-sugar-added marinara sauce (I used Monte Bene Tomato Basil Pasta Sauce)

2 ounces crumbled goat cheese (½ cup)

Place an oven rack in the bottom position. Preheat the oven to 450°F.

In a medium mixing bowl, mix the turkey, fennel, parsley, pepper flakes, Italian seasoning, and garlic powder until well combined. Set aside.

Lightly mist a medium nonstick skillet with spray. Place it over medium heat. Add the peppers and cook, stirring occasionally, for 4 to 6 minutes, or until tender. Remove the peppers from the pan and set them aside. Mist the pan again with spray, turn the heat to medium high, and add the turkey mixture. Cook the turkey, breaking it into bite-size chunks (do not crumble it), for 4 to 6 minutes, or until no longer pink.

Meanwhile press out the dough into a 14" nonstick pizza pan (do not add oil or flour or anything to the pan), being careful not to create any holes. Spread the marinara sauce evenly over all but the outer ½" diameter. Sprinkle half of the peppers, half of the turkey mixture, then the remaining peppers and the

(continued)

remaining turkey mixture evenly over the sauce. Sprinkle the cheese evenly over the top. Bake for 11 to 15 minutes, or until the crust is crisp and the cheese is melted. Allow the pizza to cool for 5 minutes, then transfer it to a cutting board (as not to ruin your nonstick pan) and cut it into 8 equal wedges. Serve immediately.

Makes 4 servings

Note: *The pizza dough I use does not say "low-fat" or "all-natural" on the front of the label, but it is. It has 1.5 grams of fat per 2-ounce serving, and the ingredient list reads "unbleached wheat flour, whole wheat flour, filtered water, canola olive oil blend, sea salt and fresh yeast."*

Per serving (2 slices): 421 calories, 33 g protein, 53 g carbohydrates (3 g sugar), 8 g fat, 2 g saturated fat, 40 mg cholesterol, 8 g fiber, 677 mg sodium

Irene Alvarado

Keep good, positive people around you. If you are constantly surrounding yourself with positive energy, you are bound to do great things. Your quality of life isn't solely based on your physical condition.

SOPHIA FRANKLIN'S "WHITE PIZZA"

This dish is very low in calories, so eating just one "pizza" is more of a snack-size serving; eat two of them if you want to make it a meal. When shopping for the fat-free ricotta cheese, always look for a brand that is all-natural, and, if you have options, choose the one lowest in sodium.

Olive oil spray (propellant free)

1 large portobello mushroom cap, rubbed clean with a damp paper towel

Sea salt, to taste

Ground black pepper, to taste

¼ cup all-natural fat-free ricotta cheese

1 teaspoon freshly minced garlic

¼ teaspoon dried oregano

8 baby spinach leaves

1½ tablespoons freshly grated all-natural Parmesan cheese

Preheat the oven to 425°F. Line a small baking sheet with foil and lightly mist the foil with spray. Lightly mist both sides of the mushroom cap with spray. Season the mushroom on both sides with salt and pepper.

Place a small nonstick skillet over medium-high heat. When hot, add the mushroom to the pan. Cook for 3 to 4 minutes per side, or until the mushroom is lightly browned and mostly tender throughout. Place the mushroom cap on the prepared baking sheet, gills side up.

In a small bowl, stir together the ricotta, garlic, and oregano until well combined. Season with salt and pepper.

Lay the spinach leaves evenly over the mushroom cap. Dollop the ricotta mixture over the spinach layer and, using the back of a spoon, spread it into an even layer. Sprinkle the Parmesan evenly over the top. Bake for 11 to 14 minutes, or until the cheese is hot throughout and lightly browned on top. Serve immediately.

Makes 1 serving

Per serving: **102 calories, 11 g protein, 7 g carbohydrates (4 g sugar), 3 g fat, 2 g saturated fat, 8 mg cholesterol, 2 g fiber, 95 mg sodium**

SPAGHETTI & MEATBALLS

Be sure to finely mince the onion as there is a lot of it in this recipe and you don't want to bite down on a big chunk. Do this by hand—never chop onions in a food processor, as the extreme overcutting that can't help but occur makes onions taste sour.

I like to buy a fresh chunk of Parmesan cheese and grate it myself. The flavor will be much stronger than that of the grocery store brands that you buy pregrated.

Olive oil spray (propellant free)

½ cup all-natural whole wheat panko style bread crumbs

2 cups loosely packed fresh parsley leaves

¼ cup unsweetened plain almond milk

1 large egg white

¾ cup minced sweet onion

¼ teaspoon sea salt

⅛ teaspoon ground black pepper

1 pound 96% lean ground beef

3 cups all-natural low-fat, low-salt, no-sugar-added marinara sauce (I used Monte Bene Tomato Basil Pasta Sauce)

6 ounces dry whole wheat or whole grain spaghetti

4 teaspoons freshly grated all-natural Parmesan cheese

Preheat the oven to 400°F. Lightly mist a large nonstick baking sheet with spray.

To the bowl of a food processor fitted with a chopping blade, add the bread crumbs and parsley. Process until they are chopped finely, stopping to scrape down the sides of the bowl, as needed. Transfer the mixture to a medium mixing bowl and stir in the milk and egg white. Add the onion, salt, pepper, and ground beef and mix until well combined. Divide the mixture into 12 equal portions and roll each into a ball. Place the meatballs side by side, so they do not touch on the prepared baking sheet. Bake for 10 to 12 minutes, or until just barely pink inside.

Meanwhile, add the marinara sauce to a medium nonstick saucepan with a lid and heat over medium heat, stirring often, until hot. Then turn the heat to low.

Cook the spaghetti according to package directions, omitting any oil or butter.

(continued)

When the meatballs are cooked, add them to the sauce and stir with a wooden spoon to coat them.

When the pasta is cooked, divide it among 4 pasta bowls. Add 3 meatballs to each bowl, then divide the sauce evenly among them. Top each with 1 teaspoon of the Parmesan.

Makes 4 servings

Per serving: 398 calories, 33 g protein, 49 g carbohydrates (6 g sugar), 9 g fat, 2 g saturated fat, 62 mg cholesterol, 9 g fiber, 518 mg sodium

Trainer Tip: Brett Hoebel

You booze, you lose. Drinking too much alcohol or drinking too often is an easy way to pack on the pounds. Keeping track of how much you drink in a night, and limiting it to a certain amount, is a good way to keep yourself in check. Order wine by the glass instead of the bottle, so you don't lose track of how much you've had.

THREE CHEESE SPINACH LASAGNA

If you're not a huge fan of spinach, but you're looking for a way to incorporate more of this nutrient-packed leafy green into your diet, this recipe is perfect for you. The spinach flavor is extremely mild, but you'll still get all of the health benefits of this nutrient-packed leafy green. Just be sure to really squeeze the spinach well to remove all the excess moisture. Otherwise, you'll end up with a soggy lasagna.

1 teaspoon extra-virgin olive oil

14 dry whole wheat lasagna noodles

1 package (12 ounces) frozen chopped spinach, thawed

3 cups all-natural fat-free ricotta cheese, drained of any liquid on top of the container

3 large egg whites

¼ cup freshly grated Parmesan cheese

2 tablespoons finely chopped fresh parsley leaves

1 teaspoon garlic powder

Sea salt, to taste

Ground black pepper, to taste

2½ cups all-natural low-fat, low-salt, no-sugar-added marinara sauce (I used Monte Bene Tomato Basil Pasta Sauce)

4 ounces finely shredded almond mozzarella cheese (I used Lisanatti)

Preheat the oven to 350°F. Bring a large pot of salted water to a boil.

Once the water is boiling, add the olive oil to the pot. Add the noodles to the pot and cook, stirring occasionally, for 8 to 10 minutes, or until al dente. Drain well. Cut or tear 2 of the noodles in half widthwise.

Meanwhile, drain the spinach well by squeezing it in a clean, lint-free dish towel until all of the excess moisture is removed. Once you think all of the moisture is removed, continue squeezing the spinach even more to ensure it is completely dry. In a medium bowl, stir together the ricotta, egg whites, 3 tablespoons of the Parmesan, parsley, and garlic powder until well combined. Stir in the drained spinach until well combined. Season with salt and pepper.

To assemble the lasagna, spread ½ cup of the marinara sauce evenly over the bottom of a 9" x 13" glass or ceramic baking dish. Lay 3½ noodles evenly across the bottom of the dish in a single layer. Dollop one-third of the ricotta mixture in big spoonfuls across the noodle layer and, using a rubber spatula, spread it

(continued)

into an even layer. Top the ricotta with ½ cup of the remaining sauce. Sprinkle one-quarter of the mozzarella evenly over the sauce. Repeat this layering process (noodles, ricotta mixture, sauce, mozzarella) two more times. For the final layer, top the lasagna with the last of the noodles. Spread the remaining sauce evenly over the noodles. Sprinkle with the remaining mozzarella, then the remaining Parmesan.

Cover the dish with foil and bake for 30 minutes. Uncover and bake for 5 to 10 minutes longer, or until the cheese is melted and the lasagna is hot throughout. Allow to cool for 5 minutes. Cut into 8 squares and serve.

Makes 8 servings

Per serving: **257 calories, 22 g protein, 34 g carbohydrates (6 g sugar), 4 g fat, <1 g saturated fat, 3 mg cholesterol, 7 g fiber, 353 mg sodium**

Moses Kinikini

Think of two or three people in your life who motivate you to be a better person. Say their names out loud while pushing through the toughest part of your workout.

SAUSAGE MUSHROOM PENNE

It's very important when eating pasta to serve it in a bowl, preferably a spaghetti bowl (the shallow bowl with the rim), in order for your eyes to enjoy it as much as your stomach. If you're anything like me, if you saw it on a plate, you'd serve yourself more before you even started eating, certain that it would never fill you. But by the time you get to the bottom of a bowl, you'd be surprised how filling it is, especially because it packs 6 grams of fiber per serving.

Olive oil spray (propellant free)

12 ounces nitrate-free, preservative-free Sweet Italian Chicken or Turkey Sausage (I used Applegate Organics Sweet Italian Chicken & Turkey Sausage), cut into ¼"-thick rounds on the diagonal

8 ounces sliced button mushrooms

½ cup dry red wine (such as Cabernet Sauvignon)

2 cups all-natural low-fat, low-salt, no-sugar-added marinara sauce (I used Monte Bene Tomato Basil Pasta Sauce)

6 ounces dry whole wheat penne

4 teaspoons freshly grated all-natural Parmesan cheese

Fresh basil leaves, cut into slivers (optional)

1 teaspoon crushed red pepper flakes (optional)

Place a large nonstick saucepan or soup pot with a lid over medium-high heat. When hot, lightly mist the pan with spray and add the sausage. Cook, stirring occasionally, for 2 to 4 minutes, or until the outsides are lightly browned. Remove the sausage to a bowl.

Mist the pan again with spray and place it back over the heat. Add the mushrooms and cook, stirring occasionally, for 4 to 6 minutes, or until tender and most of the liquid is evaporated. Add the wine and continue cooking for 2 to 4 minutes longer, or until it evaporates by about half. Add the sausage back to the pan, then add the marinara sauce. Allow the mixture to come to a simmer, then reduce the heat to low. Cover the pan and continue cooking, stirring occasionally, for at least 1 hour.

Meanwhile, prepare the pasta according to package directions.

Divide the pasta among 4 serving bowls. Divide the sauce evenly among the bowls (about 1 cup on each) and sprinkle 1 teaspoon of the Parmesan over each bowl. If desired, top with basil slivers and pepper flakes. Serve immediately.

Makes 4 servings

Per serving: 374 calories, 24 g protein, 41 g carbohydrates (6 g sugar), 9 g fat, 2 g saturated fat, 72 mg cholesterol, 6 g fiber, 715 mg sodium

CREAMY BROCCOLI PESTO PASTA WITH GRILLED CHICKEN

Freshly made, steaming hot pasta will reheat the pesto if it's at room temperature. If the pasta isn't piping hot or the pesto has been chilled, heat the pesto in the microwave or in a saucepan over low heat, stirring often, until it is hot.

9 ounces dry whole wheat pasta shells

1½ cups Broccoli Pesto (page 208), reheated if cold

1½ pounds sliced Essential Grilled Chicken (page 205), reheated if necessary

18 cherry tomatoes, cut in half

Cook the pasta according to package directions. Add the cooked pasta and the pesto to a large glass or plastic mixing bowl. Toss until the pasta is coated with the pesto. Divide the pasta evenly among 6 serving bowls. Top each bowl with one-sixth of the chicken, followed by one-sixth of the tomato halves. Serve immediately.

Makes 6 servings

Per serving: **331 calories, 36 g protein, 38 g carbohydrates (3 g sugar), 5 g fat, <1 g saturated fat, 67 mg cholesterol, 6 g fiber, 260 mg sodium**

CHICKEN CACCIATORE

This rich and satisfying dish contains a whopping 28 grams of protein and only 3 grams of fat! It really benefits from the addition of a little extra salt for optimal flavor. Add as little as possible, according to your taste.

2 teaspoons whole grain oat flour

¼ teaspoon sea salt, plus more to taste

¼ teaspoon ground black pepper, plus more to taste

4 (4-ounce) trimmed boneless, skinless chicken breasts, pounded to ½" thickness

1 teaspoon extra-virgin olive oil

1½ cups chopped sweet onion

1 cup red bell pepper strips, about 3" long and ¼"–½" wide

2 teaspoons freshly minced garlic

½ cup dry white wine

1 can (14½ ounces) all-natural no-salt-added diced tomatoes in juice

1 tablespoon all-natural drained capers

1 teaspoon dried basil

½ teaspoon dried oregano

Combine the flour, salt, and pepper on a dinner plate and use a fork to mix until they are well combined.

Pat the chicken breasts dry with a paper towel. Dip one breast at a time into the flour mixture and coat on all sides, being sure to shake off any excess flour. Transfer them, side by side, to a clean dinner plate (don't stack them on top of each other).

Place a large nonstick skillet with a lid over medium-high heat. When hot, add the olive oil. Immediately add the chicken in a single layer and cook for 2 to 3 minutes per side, or until golden brown. Remove the chicken to a plate. Add the onion, bell pepper, garlic, and wine to the pan. Stir for 3 to 5 minutes, or until the wine reduces slightly. Add the tomatoes, capers, basil, and oregano and stir to combine.

Place the chicken breasts in the sauce, completely coating them. Bring the sauce to a simmer. Cover the pan, reduce the heat to medium-low, and cook for 20 to 25 minutes, or until the chicken is tender and no longer pink. Season with salt and pepper. Serve.

Makes 4 servings

Per serving (1 chicken breast + ¾ cup sauce): **219 calories, 28 g protein, 13 g carbohydrates (4 g sugar), 3 g fat, <1 g saturated fat, 66 mg cholesterol, 3 g fiber, 260 mg sodium**

4

Asian and Southeast Asian Flavors

It's not a good idea to talk to Chef Devin on an empty stomach. When she starts to describe the recipes she's created for this chapter—such as Crispy Pork Wontons (page 59), Shrimp Toasts (page 65), and Yakitori Beef Skewers (page 86), which she says "taste super fattening"—your mouth is sure to water.

As any fan of Asian takeout knows, most items on the menu are far from healthy and go heavy on the oil, sodium, and portion sizes. But as usual, we've found a way to create the flavors you crave without breaking your calorie budget. Chef Devin uses wholesome ingredients such as fresh vegetables, healthy proteins, Ezekiel bread, and herbs and spices to re-create your favorite dishes with a fraction of the fat and calories you'll find on any takeout menu.

Chinese food isn't the only ethnic cuisine you'll sample in these pages. You'll also find recipes for Japanese food, Thai food, Indian food, and even Tongan food. Who can forget the dramatic transformations (and charming personalities) of Tongan contestants in Season 7, Sione and Filipe Fa, and Season 9, Sam and Koli Palu? Sione, who contributed a recipe to this chapter, says that most Tongan dishes are full of fatty meats and oils. His revamped pork recipe is a much healthier version of the traditional Tongan dish and delivers wonderfully exotic flavors.

While most people tend to think of Japanese food as healthy (and if prepared correctly, it is), there can be as many as 600 calories in the specialty sushi rolls you'll find at many restaurants. The sushi dishes in this chapter are much truer to the traditional ingredients in Japanese cuisine—fresh fish, a little rice, and plenty of vegetables. Salmon and tuna, which are go-to proteins in Japanese cuisine, are rich sources of heart-healthy omega-3 fats. And if you're not a fan of raw fish, Chef Devin has even created a recipe for "sushi virgins," which uses cooked fish to make a delicious roll.

If you do go out for Asian food, *Biggest Loser* Club nutrition expert Louise Massey, RD, says that sushi can be a good option because "the presentation makes it easier to eat slowly." Just be sure to choose simple rolls that contain fish and vegetables, and order brown rice when available. And steer clear of anything that's been fried (avoid the word *tempura*) and "spicy" rolls smothered in mayonnaise sauce. Opt for healthy side dishes like edamame (½ cup has about 100 calories) and seaweed salad (about 70 calories per serving).

If you've never tried making Asian food at home, now's the time to start. It's easier than you think to bring flavors from around the world into your very own kitchen. Now let's get cooking!

Trainer Tip: Jillian Michaels

It's a common myth that when you quit smoking, you pack on the pounds. Studies show that people who exercise while quitting smoking have a higher success rate at staying smoke-free in the long run. Former smokers lose weight just as effectively as nonsmokers. So put down that cigarette and hit the gym.

CRISPY PORK WONTONS

The Biggest Loser *contestants and I love to serve these wontons along with the Chinese Chicken Chop Salad (page 62) and Shrimp Toasts (page 65) when hosting friends to watch the show.*

Use a good nonstick baking sheet for these wontons. If you don't have one, line a baking sheet with nonstick foil or a silicone baking mat. Because the oven temperature is so high, it's best not to use parchment paper. If you are using more than one baking sheet, place them side by side in your oven to ensure even browning.

Olive oil spray (propellant free)

⅛ cup canned, all-natural, drained and sliced water chestnuts

1 medium carrot, peeled, trimmed, and cut into 6 equal pieces

4 medium whole scallions, trimmed and cut into thirds

8 ounces extra-lean ground pork

½ tablespoon dry sherry

1 tablespoon all-natural egg substitute

½ tablespoon hot toasted sesame oil

Pinch salt

Pinch ground black pepper

24 (about 3"-square) all-natural wheat wonton wrappers (I used Nasoya Won Ton Wraps), see note on page 61

All-natural hot mustard for dipping (optional)

Place an oven rack in the lowest position in the oven. Preheat the oven to 450°F. Lightly mist a large nonstick baking sheet with spray.

Place the water chestnuts, carrot, and scallions in the bowl of a food processor fitted with a chopping blade. Process until the ingredients are minced, stopping to scrape down the sides of the bowl intermittently, if necessary. Put the chopped vegetables in a fine mesh strainer. Using a rubber spatula or a spoon, press out any moisture. Transfer the drained veggies to a medium glass or plastic mixing bowl and add the pork, sherry, egg substitute, oil, salt, and pepper. With a fork or clean hands, mix the ingredients until well combined.

Fill a small bowl with cold water.

Place a wonton wrapper on a clean, flat work surface. Spoon 1 tablespoon of the filling into the center of the wrapper. Dip your finger in the water and run your fingertip along two adjoining edges of the wrapper. Fold the wrapper in half diagonally, creating a triangle. Gently press your finger around the edges of the wrapper, sealing the dry side to the moistened side, being careful not to leave any air bubbles. Press on the filling slightly to spread it out (if the mound of filling in the center is too thick, the wontons won't cook evenly).

Transfer the wonton to the prepared baking sheet. Continue filling and sealing the remaining wonton wrappers, until all of the filling

(continued)

mixture and wrappers are used. Working in batches if necessary, place all the finished wontons on the baking sheet in a single layer, so they do not touch.

Lightly mist the tops of the wontons with spray and bake for 5 minutes on the lower oven rack. Gently flip them, mist the tops again with spray, and bake for 3 to 5 minutes longer, or until the outsides are lightly browned and the pork is no longer pink, being careful not to burn the edges of the wontons. Serve immediately with mustard for dipping, if desired.

Makes 4 servings

Note: *You may need a few more than 24 wonton wrappers, as the volume of the filling as well as the precision of measuring each tablespoon can vary slightly. Nutritional data is based on using all of the filling in the 24 wrappers.*

Per serving (6 wontons): **228 calories, 19 g protein, 26 g carbohydrates (2 g sugar), 4 g fat, <1 g saturated fat, 45 mg cholesterol, 2 g fiber, 369 mg sodium**

Sarah Nitta

Ignore the chatter in your head that tells you all the reasons to quit. That chatter is simply fear that's telling you that you can't be who you want to be. Believing in yourself changes everything. I used to believe that I was weak, but I have learned that I am so much more than I was allowing myself to be.

CHINESE CHICKEN CHOP SALAD

If you really want a restaurant-style salad, be sure to blot the excess moisture from your lettuce, which can water down the dressing and make the salad soggy. I like to arrange the orange wedges around the plate for an extra special presentation when I serve this dish at home, but for a lunch on the go, you could assemble the salad in a resealable plastic container, keeping the oranges and the dressing separate. Healthy Chinese "takeout" at a fraction of the price! You'll be the envy of all your co-workers.

2 cups loosely packed shredded romaine lettuce

1½ cups loosely packed shredded Napa cabbage

⅓ cup slivered carrots

⅓ cup finely chopped whole scallions

⅓ cup mung bean sprouts

3 tablespoons all-natural, no-sugar-added Chinese dressing (I used Follow Your Heart Fresh and Natural Sesame Miso Dressing)

4 ounces sliced Essential Grilled Chicken (page 205)

12 canned (in juice or water, not syrup) mandarin orange sections, drained (about ⅓ cup)

In a medium mixing bowl, toss together the lettuce, cabbage, carrots, scallions, sprouts, and dressing. Mound the mixture on a serving plate and top with the chicken. Place the oranges evenly around edges of the plate.

Makes 1 serving

Per serving: 324 calories, 32 g protein, 25 g carbohydrates (15 g sugar), 11 g fat, 2 g saturated fat, 66 mg cholesterol, 7 g fiber, 366 mg sodium

SHRIMP TOASTS

Have you ever been to a dim sum restaurant? If so, you've probably had shrimp toasts. Most of the time, this popular menu item is deep-fried and contains more filler than shrimp. This version is a tasty alternative that's full of real shrimp.

Note that if the bread you are using isn't perfectly square, you should cut the slices as close to the edges as possible to remove crusts (if a little bit remains, it's okay).

3   slices all-natural sesame sprouted grain bread (no more than 80 calories per slice; I used Ezekiel 4:9 brand)

3   medium whole scallions, chopped into 2"-long pieces

1   piece (1") peeled fresh ginger

2   medium cloves fresh garlic

12   ounces medium (51–60 count) peeled and deveined shrimp (approximately 1 pound unpeeled)

1   tablespoon all-natural egg substitute

⅛   teaspoon salt

Pinch ground black pepper

1   tablespoon sesame seeds

Olive oil spray (propellant-free)

Preheat the oven to 400°F.

Place the bread slices side by side on a small nonstick baking sheet. Bake for 1 to 2 minutes, or until light golden brown on top. Flip the slices and bake for 1 to 2 minutes longer, or until light golden brown on top. Transfer the toasted bread to a cutting board.

Reduce the oven temperature to 350°F.

Place the scallions, ginger, and garlic in the bowl of a food processor fitted with a chopping blade. Process the mixture until minced, then remove it to a medium glass or plastic mixing bowl. Add the shrimp, egg substitute, salt, and pepper and process until some small chunks of shrimp remain (it shouldn't be completely smooth like a paste). Add the shrimp mixture to the chopped green onion mixture, and stir until well combined.

Spread one-third of the shrimp mixture evenly over one of the bread slices. Using a sharp knife, cut the slice into 8 triangles by cutting it in half horizontally, then vertically, and then across both diagonals. Repeat with the remaining bread slices and shrimp mixture.

Place the toast triangles on the same prepared baking sheet in a single layer. Sprinkle the sesame seeds evenly over each toast. Lightly mist

(continued)

the tops of the shrimp toasts with spray. Bake for 17 to 20 minutes, or until the shrimp mixture is cooked through and no longer pink inside. Serve immediately.

Makes 8 servings

Per serving (3 toasts): **78 calories, 10 g protein, 5 g carbohydrates (trace sugar), 1 g fat, trace saturated fat, 65 mg cholesterol, 1 g fiber, 127 mg sodium**

Ken Andrews

Try to eat a little protein with every meal and snack. It helps to prevent your blood sugar from spiking, which makes you hungry.

SPICY SZECHUAN EGGPLANT

Though I love the authentic flavor and texture of Chinese eggplant for this dish, you can use any variety of eggplant you like. Chinese and Japanese eggplants tend to have a slightly thinner skin than traditional, larger eggplant, but this dish cooks long enough for any variety of eggplant to become tender. Very large eggplants (of any variety) are usually older than the smaller ones and may be slightly bitter. So don't buy the biggest eggplant you see at the store!

1 teaspoon cornstarch

¼ cup all-natural low-sodium vegetable broth

1½ tablespoons all-natural lower-sodium soy sauce

1 tablespoon rice vinegar

½ tablespoon freshly squeezed lemon juice

1 tablespoon light agave nectar

¼ teaspoon crushed red pepper flakes, or more to taste

1 teaspoon toasted or roasted sesame oil

½ cup 1" squares sweet onion

¼ cup chopped whole scallions

½ tablespoon freshly minced garlic

¾ pound Chinese eggplant, cut into ½" cubes

2 tablespoons water

1 tablespoon toasted sesame seeds

Add the cornstarch to a small mixing bowl. Whisking constantly, slowly add the broth until the cornstarch is completely dissolved. Whisk in the soy sauce, vinegar, lemon juice, agave, and pepper flakes. Set aside.

Place a large nonstick skillet or wok over medium-high heat. When hot, add the oil, onion, half of the scallions, and garlic. Cook, stirring occasionally, for 1 to 2 minutes, or until the onions begin to soften. Add the eggplant and water and continue cooking, stirring occasionally, for 6 to 9 minutes, or until the eggplant is tender and lightly browned.

Meanwhile, pour the reserved sauce mixture in a small nonstick skillet or saucepan. Place the pan over medium-high heat and cook, stirring frequently, for 1 to 3 minutes, or until it thickens slightly. When the eggplant is cooked, pour the sauce mixture over the eggplant. Immediately remove the eggplant

(continued)

from the heat and stir in the remaining scallions and the sesame seeds until well combined and the eggplant is evenly coated with sauce. Serve immediately.

Makes 2 servings

Per serving: 162 calories, 3 g protein, 27 g carbohydrates (15 g sugar),
5 g fat, trace saturated fat, 0 mg cholesterol, 7 g fiber, 373 mg sodium

Trainer Tip: Bob Harper

If you've got a lot of weight to lose, don't think about that big number. Think about what you can do today. The choices you make today can help keep you in control of your life. That's what it's about. Little feats get bigger.

SWEET & SOUR PORK

Though this dish contains a healthy dose of lean protein and veggies, it's also a bit high in carbohydrates, so it's best to skip serving it with a side of rice. Steamed broccoli or sautéed snow peas are a great substitute.

Be sure to have all of the ingredients prepped and measured before you turn on the heat. The cooking process should be done very quickly to maintain restaurant quality.

For the Stir-Fry:

1¼ pounds trimmed pork tenderloin, cut into ½" medallions

5 tablespoons rice vinegar

3 tablespoons agave nectar

2 tablespoons all-natural lower-sodium soy sauce

1½ tablespoons all-natural no-salt-added tomato paste

1 tablespoon dry sherry

1½ tablespoons cornstarch

Olive oil spray (propellant free)

3 whole scallions, trimmed and cut into 1" pieces on a diagonal

1 medium red bell pepper, cored, seeded, and cut into 1" cubes

2 tablespoons slivered fresh red chile peppers (Fresno chiles; wear plastic gloves when handling), see note

2 teaspoons freshly minced garlic

½ cup drained canned all-natural bamboo shoots

2 teaspoons avocado oil

Place the pork medallions in a single layer between 2 sheets of waxed paper, working in batches if necessary. Using the flat side of a meat mallet, pound them until they are very thin (about ⅛" thick). Cut each in half lengthwise, then transfer them to a medium bowl. Toss them in 2 tablespoons of the rice vinegar and let them marinate, covered, in the refrigerator for 20 minutes, turning them at least once.

Meanwhile, whisk together the agave, soy sauce, tomato paste, sherry, and the remaining 3 tablespoons rice vinegar in a small mixing bowl until well combined. Set the sauce aside.

Remove the pork from the vinegar and shake off any excess as you transfer the pieces to a clean medium bowl. Add the cornstarch and toss until coated evenly.

Place a large nonstick wok over high heat. When hot, lightly mist it with spray and add the scallions, bell pepper, chile peppers, garlic, and bamboo shoots. Cook, stirring frequently, for 3 to 5 minutes, or until the veggies are crisp-tender (be careful not to burn the garlic). Remove the veggies from the pan and cover to keep warm.

(continued)

Return the pan to the heat and immediately add 1 teaspoon of the avocado oil and half of the pork in a single layer. Cook, stirring frequently, until the pork is just barely pink inside. Add it to the veggie mixture. Repeat with the remaining 1 teaspoon oil and the remaining pork.

Return the cooked pork and veggies to the pan and pour the reserved sauce over the top. Turn off the heat. Stir the sauce until it thickens slightly, enough to coat the meat and veggies. Serve immediately.

Makes 4 (heaping 1-cup) servings

Note: *If you prefer a dish that is less spicy, seed the chiles. If you prefer spicier food, do not seed them.*

Per serving: **269 calories, 31 g protein, 21 g carbohydrates (15 g sugar), 6 g fat, 1 g saturated fat, 92 mg cholesterol, 1 g fiber, 315 mg sodium**

Courtney Crozier

Don't judge yourself according to others' abilities. Do what you can do, your absolute best, and then try to get better each day. If you can only walk half a mile, be proud of that and push yourself harder the next time to go a little farther.

BON-BON CHICKEN

I love serving this dish in lettuce cups when I'm looking for a super-satisfying low-carb meal. As an alternative to poaching the chicken as directed below, you can use up any leftover grilled, roasted, or baked chicken you have on hand.

2 cups all-natural low-sodium chicken broth

½ pound trimmed boneless, skinless chicken breasts

½ medium cucumber, seeded and cut into very thin strips about 2" long

1 recipe Asian Peanut Sauce (page 207)

1 whole scallion, trimmed and minced

½ teaspoon toasted sesame seeds

Add the broth to a medium saucepan big enough to accommodate the broth covering the chicken breasts by at least 1". Place the saucepan over high heat. When the broth comes to a boil, add the chicken, turn the heat to a simmer, and poach the chicken in the liquid (see note), uncovered, for 6 to 8 minutes, or until no longer pink inside. Drain the chicken from the liquid and allow it to cool to room temperature. Then refrigerate it until chilled, if desired.

When the chicken is completely cooled (or chilled), use your fingers to pull it apart, creating small shreds. Mound the shreds in the center of 2 plates. Sprinkle the cucumber evenly around the chicken, along the edge of the plate. Pour the sauce evenly in the center. Top it with the scallions, then the sesame seeds, and serve.

Makes 2 servings

Note: *If the chicken is not covered by the broth either when it's originally added or during cooking, add enough water to the broth so that it is covered.*

Per serving: 254 calories, 31 g protein, 10 g carbohydrates (5 g sugar), 9 g fat, 1 g saturated fat, 66 mg cholesterol, 2 g fiber, 338 mg sodium

ORANGE CHICKEN

I'm sure the temptation is to serve this dish over rice. That said, due to the cornstarch and orange juice, this dish, like the traditional version from your local Chinese takeout, provides almost as many carbohydrates as ½ cup of cooked rice. So it's best to enjoy this with a side of steamed broccoli or some roasted green beans, to keep your meal balanced.

For the chicken:

- 4 (4-ounce) trimmed boneless, skinless chicken breasts
- ⅛ teaspoon salt
- Ground black pepper, to taste
- 2 teaspoons cornstarch
- ½ teaspoon Chinese five-spice powder (look for it in the spice aisle)

For the sauce:

- ½ cup 100% orange juice (not from concentrate)
- 2 tablespoons rice vinegar
- 2 tablespoons + 2 teaspoons all-natural lower-sodium soy sauce
- 1 tablespoon honey
- 1 tablespoon + 1 teaspoon toasted or roasted sesame oil
- 1 tablespoon + 1 teaspoon cornstarch

For the stir-fry:

- Olive oil spray (propellant free)
- 4 small cloves fresh garlic, minced
- 2 dried red chile peppers, minced (wear plastic gloves when handling)
- 1½ cups 1" squares red onion
- 1 red bell pepper, cut into 1" squares
- 1 yellow bell pepper, cut into 1" squares
- 1 tablespoon minced peeled fresh ginger
- 1 cup snow peas, ends trimmed
- Zest of 1 orange

To make the chicken: Place the chicken breasts between two sheets of waxed paper or plastic wrap on a cutting board. Using the flat end of a meat mallet, pound the chicken to an even ¼" thickness. Cut the chicken breasts in half lengthwise, yielding 8 pieces of chicken. Cut each piece into ½"-thick strips on the diagonal. Transfer the strips to a large bowl and season with salt and pepper. Add the 2 teaspoons cornstarch and the five-spice powder and toss until the chicken is evenly coated.

(continued)

To make the sauce: In a small bowl, whisk together the orange juice, rice vinegar, soy sauce, honey, sesame oil, and cornstarch.

To make the stir-fry: Place a medium nonstick wok or skillet over high heat. When hot, lightly mist it with spray. Add half of the chicken in a single layer, not touching, and cook for 2 to 3 minutes, stirring occasionally, until cooked through and no longer pink inside. Transfer it to a bowl and cover to keep warm. Mist the pan again with spray and repeat with the remaining chicken. Remove it to the bowl to keep warm.

Respray the pan and add the garlic, chile peppers, onion, bell peppers, ginger, and snow peas. Cook, stirring occasionally, for 2 minutes, or until the veggies turn a brighter shade. Add the sauce and the chicken back to the pan. Continue cooking for 1 to 2 minutes, or until the sauce has thickened. Transfer to a serving bowl and top with the zest. Serve immediately.

Makes 4 (1¼-cup) servings

Per serving: **282 calories, 29 g protein, 26 g carbohydrates (13 g sugar), 7 g fat, 1 g saturated fat, 66 mg cholesterol, 3 g fiber, 460 mg sodium**

Kaylee Kinikini

Give 100 percent each time you work out. Train hard and you will burn more calories in a shorter amount of time. Fifty percent effort doesn't work for weight loss! When you push yourself past your limits, you'll discover what you are truly capable of.

JAPANESE CUCUMBER SALAD

Scraping out the seeds from the cucumber is a very important step because it keeps this salad from becoming watery. Another important step in preparing this simple yet refreshing salad is to allow the flavors to meld overnight in the fridge—it makes all the difference in the overall taste.

2 medium cucumbers, peeled and seeded

¾ cup unseasoned rice vinegar

1 cup cold water

2 tablespoons light agave nectar

⅛ teaspoon salt, or to taste

1 teaspoon toasted sesame seeds or black sesame seeds (optional)

Cut the cucumbers in half lengthwise. Using a small spoon, gently scrape out the seeds. Cut the cucumbers into ¼"-thick half-moon pieces.

In a shallow, resealable plastic container (big enough that most of the cucumbers will be covered with the liquid), whisk together the vinegar, water, agave, and salt until well combined. Stir in the cucumbers (they should be at least halfway covered in the liquid). Cover and refrigerate for at least 6 hours or overnight, stirring at least once. Divide the cucumbers among 2 serving bowls and top with sesame seeds, if desired. Serve immediately.

Makes 2 servings

Per serving: 60 calories, 3 g protein, 14 g carbohydrates (11 g sugar), 0 g fat, 0 g saturated fat, 0 mg cholesterol, 3 g fiber, 75 mg sodium

DAN DAN MIAN (SPICY SZECHUAN NOODLES)

Dan Dan Mian and similar peanut noodle dishes typically have as many as 20 grams of fat and 1,638 milligrams of sodium per serving. The Biggest Loser *contestants love this much-improved version that doesn't weigh them down in calories or in spirit.*

6 ounces dry 100% whole grain udon noodles (I used Eden Organic)

1½ recipes Asian Peanut Sauce (page 207)

½ cup all-natural low-sodium chicken broth

12 ounces extra-lean ground turkey (I used Jennie-O)

2 tablespoons freshly minced garlic

2 tablespoons minced peeled fresh ginger

2 teaspoons all-natural lower-sodium soy sauce

½ cup finely chopped whole scallions

Canola oil spray (propellant free)

2 cups mung bean sprouts

Finely chopped fresh Thai green or red chiles, to taste (wear plastic gloves when handling), optional

Cook the noodles according to package directions.

In a small mixing bowl, whisk together the Asian Peanut Sauce and broth until well combined. Set aside.

In another small mixing bowl, mix the turkey, garlic, ginger, soy sauce, and ¼ cup of the scallions until well combined.

Place a large nonstick wok or skillet over high heat. When hot, mist with spray and add the turkey mixture. Cook, breaking the meat into small chunks, for 3 minutes, or until lightly browned and cooked through. Add the peanut sauce mixture and cook for 1 minute, or until just hot. Remove from the heat.

Divide the noodles among 4 bowls. Top each with one-quarter of the pork and sauce mixture. Top each with ½ cup of the bean sprouts. Divide the remaining ¼ cup scallions among them. Top with chiles, if desired. Serve immediately.

Makes 4 servings

Per serving: 345 calories, 32 g protein, 42 g carbohydrates (7 g sugar), 8 g fat, 1 g saturated fat, 34 mg cholesterol, 6 g fiber, 428 mg sodium

SASHIMI TUNA SALAD

Make sure the tuna you purchase for this salad is extra fresh. It should be bright red, with no discoloration. If it doesn't seem fresh at the fish counter, check the sushi area, if there is one. You may pay a bit more, but it's totally worth buying a block a sashimi-grade tuna for the fresh flavor it brings to this dish.

4 cups loosely packed mixed greens

1 cup snow peas, trimmed and cut in half horizontally

⅓ cup red bell pepper slivers, about 2" long

¼ cup red onion slivers

3 tablespoons no-sugar-added all-natural Japanese dressing (I used Follow Your Heart Organic Creamy Miso Ginger Dressing)

4 ounces sashimi or sushi-grade ahi tuna, cut into bite-size cubes

1–2 tablespoons finely cut dried seaweed (optional)

Add the mixed greens, snow peas, bell peppers, and onion to a medium mixing bowl. Drizzle the dressing over top and toss until well combined. Mound the salad onto a serving plate, leaving at least a 1½" diameter bare around the edge of the plate. Place the cubes of tuna evenly around the bare edge. Garnish with seaweed, if desired. Serve immediately.

Makes 1 serving

Per serving: 332 calories, 31 g protein, 23 g carbohydrates (11 g sugar), 12 g fat, 1 g saturated fat, 52 mg cholesterol, 7 g fiber, 424 mg sodium

SUSHI VIRGIN CUT ROLL

I call this a "sushi virgin" roll because all of the fish is cooked, so it's technically not sushi. But it does certainly look like the creative rolls that are popping up at more and more Americanized Japanese restaurants.

This is a great recipe for using up leftover roasted or grilled salmon. In fact, I always make a point of cooking extra when I'm making salmon, specifically to make this roll.

2   sheets (about 8 x 7½") nori (seaweed)

2   cups cooked short grain brown rice, cooled to room temperature

4   ounces roasted or grilled wild-caught salmon, skin removed

4   ounces lump crabmeat

10   paper-thin lemon slices (rounds)

½   small jalapeño pepper, cut into slivers, or to taste (wear plastic gloves when handling)

2   tablespoons fresh cilantro leaves

  Prepared wasabi (optional)

  Lemon wedges

1   tablespoon all-natural lower-sodium soy sauce (optional)

Place a sushi mat on a work surface so that the wooden sticks that comprise it run horizontally. Place 1 sheet of nori on the sushi mat. Run your hands under cool water, then shake them, so that they're barely wet. Using your hands, scatter 1 cup of the rice evenly over the nori, all the way to the edges. Press the rice firmly in a thin, even layer so the nori is completely covered. (Remoisten your hands slightly if the rice starts to stick to them).

Lay half of the salmon in a line to cover the inch or two that runs horizontally closest to you. Lay half of the crab in a horizontal strip just above the salmon mixture. Lay 5 of the lemon slices evenly over the salmon. Lay half of the jalapeño, then 1 tablespoon of the cilantro evenly over the crab. Put a touch of wasabi, if desired, on the tip of your finger and run it across the rice just above the crab.

Pick up the end of the sushi mat and nori closest to you and roll it tightly to the rice on the far side. Continue to roll it so that the exposed rice wraps around the stuffed roll, making sure not to roll the mat into the roll. Transfer the roll to a cutting board.

Run a very sharp knife with a thin, straight blade under cold water. Shake off any excess water, then slice the roll into 12 thin, equal slices.

Repeat the procedure, using the remaining nori, rice, salmon, crab, lemon, jalapeño, and cilantro. Serve with plenty of lemon wedges for squeezing and soy sauce, if desired.

Makes 4 (¹/₂-roll) servings

Per serving: **199 calories, 14 g protein, 28 g carbohydrates (trace sugar), 5 g fat, <1 g saturated fat, 37 mg cholesterol, 2 g fiber, 146 mg sodium**

Don Evans

Do it for yourself and the things that define you, such as being a husband, a father, a brother, and a son. You can accomplish so much more than you thought you could.

RICELESS SPICY TUNA ROLL

You may want to buy extra cucumbers—it could take a few tries to make the perfect cucumber "wrappers." If you really have trouble or don't want to practice, you can always peel the cucumber with a veggie peeler, trim the ends, then cut the cucumber into 4 pieces crosswise and hollow out the centers using a grapefruit knife. Then simply stuff the pieces before slicing each into 3 sushi-size pieces (you'll also want to use 8 smaller slices of avocado instead of the 6 below). The cucumber will be thicker than the paper wrappers but definitely still tasty.

2 large cucumbers (10–12 ounces each; look for cucumbers with an even shape and thickness)

8 ounces sashimi or sushi-grade ahi tuna, cut into ¼" pieces

½ teaspoon hot chili oil

Sea salt, to taste

1¼ ounces avocado, cut lengthwise into 6 equal strips

All-natural wasabi (optional)

All-natural ponzu sauce for dipping (optional), see note

Using a very sharp knife, cut the ends off the cucumbers and peel them. Then cut them in thirds crosswise. To make a thin, nori-like "wrapper," set 1 piece of the cucumber on a clean work surface on its side. Begin by carefully making the thinnest cut possible along the outside of the cucumber, starting at the top cutting about 90 degrees, then rotating the cucumber to continue cutting a long "sheet," until you rotate enough to hit the seeds in the center and have a long cucumber "sheet."

In a small bowl, mix the tuna with the oil until well combined. Season with sea salt.

Place one-third of the tuna on one end of the cucumber "wrapper." Add 1 slice of avocado and spread a little bit of wasabi across it, if desired. Carefully roll the cucumber until you reach the opposite end. Repeat with the remaining pieces of cucumber, ahi, and avocado. Then slice each section into 4 sushi roll pieces. Serve with wasabi and/or ponzu sauce, if desired, or sprinkle with additional sea salt, to taste.

Makes 2 servings

Note: *Ponzu sauce is a citrus-based soy sauce found in many natural food stores. Be sure to use it in moderation, as there are about 450 milligrams of sodium in 1 tablespoon of even reduced-sodium varieties.*

Per serving: 179 calories, 28 g protein, 5 g carbohydrates (2 g sugar), 5 g fat, <1 g saturated fat, 52 mg cholesterol, 2 g fiber, 47 mg sodium

YAKITORI BEEF SKEWERS

The literal translation of yakitori is "grilled bird," so you'll often see this Japanese dish made from various parts of chicken (chicken thighs, breast, livers, and even skin)—though many Japanese-American versions of yakitori are made with other types of meat besides chicken. I like using ground beef because it's so easy (no trimming required), and I can mix up the meat in advance and pop the skewers on the grill when I'm ready.

I recommend using 6" skewers, but these tasty bites are just as delicious no matter what size of skewer you use!

1 pound 96% lean ground beef, preferably grass fed

1 teaspoon freshly minced garlic

1 teaspoon minced peeled fresh ginger

2 teaspoons finely chopped whole scallions

1 tablespoon + 1 teaspoon all-natural low-sodium soy sauce

Sea salt, to taste

All-natural, no-sugar-added Japanese dressing (I used Follow Your Heart Organic Creamy Miso Ginger Dressing), optional (see note)

Soak 8 (6") wooden skewers in water for at least 30 minutes (or have metal skewers ready). Preheat a grill to high.

Add the beef, garlic, ginger, scallions, and soy sauce to a medium bowl. Mix well to combine. Season with salt.

Divide the mixture into 8 equal portions. Take 1 portion and shape it around a skewer, flattening the meat so it's about 1½" wide and covers about 5" of the skewer's length. Place the finished skewer on a dinner plate. Repeat with the remaining meat mixture and skewers. Transfer the plate to the freezer and let the skewers sit about 10 minutes.

Grill the skewers for 2 to 3 minutes per side, or until the meat is cooked through and no longer pink. Divide the yakitori among 4 serving plates, and serve immediately, alongside the dressing for dipping, if desired.

Makes 4 servings

Note: *Be careful not to overdo the dressing or the dipping. Each tablespoon of my suggested dressing adds 40 calories, 3.5 grams of fat, and 120 milligrams of sodium.*

Per serving (2 skewers): 135 calories, 23 g protein, <1 g carbohydrates (trace sugar), 5 g fat, 2 g saturated fat, 60 mg cholesterol, trace fiber, 196 mg sodium

THAI BEEF PAPAYA SALAD

Fish sauce is a common ingredient in many Southeast Asian dishes. It's made from fish that have been fermented and has a very strong, distinct flavor that is essential to a lot of recipes, including this salad. You'll notice I use a small amount in this recipe—it's high in sodium, so I recommend using it sparingly.

- ¼ teaspoon olive oil
- 4 ounces trimmed top round steak, preferably grass fed
- 1 teaspoon all-natural salt-free Thai seasoning (I used The Spice Hunter Salt Free Thai Seasoning Blend)
- 2 tablespoons freshly squeezed lime juice
- 1½ teaspoons grated fresh lemongrass stalk

- ½ teaspoon all-natural fish sauce
- 1 teaspoon coconut sugar
- ⅓ cup thin, bite-size strips fresh papaya
- ½ medium cucumber, seeded and cut into matchsticks
- ¼ cup red onion slivers
- 1 tablespoon chopped fresh mint leaves, or more to taste

- 1 tablespoon chopped fresh cilantro leaves
- 2 teaspoons finely slivered fresh red chile peppers (Fresno chiles; wear plastic gloves when handling), see note
- 3 cups mixed baby greens

Preheat a grill to high.

Rub the oil evenly over the steak, then rub the seasoning evenly over the steak. Let it stand until the grill is hot.

Meanwhile, in a small bowl, whisk together the lime juice, lemongrass, fish sauce, and sugar.

Grill the steak for 1 to 2 minutes per side for medium rare. Transfer to a plate, tent with foil, and let sit for 10 minutes while the juices redistribute.

In a large serving bowl, combine the papaya, cucumber, onion, mint, cilantro, and chiles. Slice the steak and add it to the bowl. Add the lime juice dressing and toss until well combined.

(continued)

Spread the greens evenly over a dinner plate. Mound the steak mixture in the center, atop the greens. Serve immediately.

Makes 1 serving

Note: *For a less spicy salad, seed the chile. If you prefer a spicier salad, don't seed it.*

Per serving: 234 calories, 29 g protein, 27 g carbohydrates (14 g sugar), 5 g fat, 2 g saturated fat, 50 mg cholesterol, 8 g fiber, 363 mg sodium

MORE FIT FISH BALLS

Steaming is a simple and healthy way to cook a variety of proteins. There are tons of commercial steamers on the market, and pot-and-pan sets often come with a steamer insert. You can also buy a bamboo steamer for an authentic experience, or if you want to save your pennies, there are plenty of steamer inserts that are very inexpensive. Regardless of what kind of steamer you have, you need to make sure that you have a pot or pan that is deep enough to hold the steamer insert and allow a tight-fitting lid to be placed on top without smashing your food.

½ pound boned tilapia filets or other white fish, preferably wild-caught, cut into 1" cubes

2 small whole scallions, trimmed and cut into 3 pieces

1 slice (1 ounce) nitrate-free turkey bacon, cut into 1" pieces

1 tablespoon all-natural reduced-sodium soy sauce

1 tablespoon all-natural egg substitute

½ tablespoon dry sherry

½ teaspoon toasted sesame oil

½ tablespoon fresh cilantro leaves, roughly chopped, or more to taste

Olive oil spray (propellant free)

Cover a clean, flat work surface with a sheet of waxed paper or parchment paper.

To the bowl of a food processor fitted with a chopping blade, add the fish, scallions, and bacon. Process, stopping to scrape down the bowl a couple of times, until relatively smooth. Transfer the mixture to a bowl and stir in the soy sauce, egg substitute, sherry, sesame oil, and cilantro until well combined. Divide the mixture into 8 portions and place them on the waxed or parchment paper. Using your hands (it might help to dampen them slightly to prevent the mixture from sticking to your hands), roll each portion into a ball.

Lightly mist a steamer rack with spray and place over (or in) a pan of boiling water. Add the fish balls, working in batches if necessary, to the steamer in a single layer so they do not touch. Cover the pan and steam them for 7 to 10 minutes, or until they are cooked through (no longer translucent in the center) and firm. Transfer them to a serving platter and top with additional cilantro, if desired. Serve immediately.

Makes 2 servings

Per serving: 158 calories, 27 g protein, 3 carbohydrates (1 g sugar), 4 g fat, <1 g saturated fat, 69 mg cholesterol, trace fiber, 407 mg sodium

TIKKA TURKEY KEBABS

Be sure that you buy turkey tenderloins, not turkey breast cubes or other cuts of turkey. The tenderloins are as lean as the turkey breast but more tender, so they yield a much better result in this preparation.

⅔ cup all-natural fat-free plain yogurt

2 tablespoons + ½ tablespoon salt-free, preservative-free Indian rub or seasoning (I used NoMU Indian Rub)

½ teaspoon + ⅛ teaspoon sea salt

20-ounce package trimmed turkey tenderloins (I used Jennie-O), cut into 24 equal pieces

½ tablespoon extra-virgin olive oil

32 (¼"-thick) zucchini rounds

32 (1") squares sweet onion

Olive oil spray (propellant free)

In a small bowl, mix together the yogurt, 2 tablespoons of the spice rub, and ½ teaspoon of the salt until well combined.

Place the turkey in a large resealable plastic container or plastic bag. Pour the yogurt mixture evenly over the turkey. Toss well to coat. Marinate overnight in the refrigerator.

Soak 8 (at least 8") wooden skewers in water for at least 30 minutes (or have metal skewers ready). When you're ready to prepare the dish, preheat a grill to high.

In a medium mixing bowl, drizzle the oil over the zucchini and onion. Sprinkle the remaining ½ tablespoon rub and ⅛ teaspoon salt over top. Toss them until well mixed.

Thread the following pieces onto one skewer: zucchini, onion, turkey, zucchini, onion, turkey, zucchini, onion, turkey, zucchini, and onion. Repeat with the remaining skewers, veggies, and turkey until you have 8 kebabs. Mist the kebabs on all sides with spray. Grill them for 2 to 3 minutes per side, or until the turkey is no longer pink inside. Serve immediately.

Makes 4 servings

Per serving (2 kebabs): **222 calories, 38 g protein, 12 g carbohydrates (6 g sugar), 4 g fat, trace saturated fat, 57 mg cholesterol, 2 g fiber, 401 mg sodium**

MINT RAITA

This Indian favorite is similar to the popular Greek yogurt dip tzatziki. It's delicious with whole wheat naan (which you can buy at many grocery stores these days; just be sure to find an all-natural one) and served as a snack or as an accompaniment to spicy dishes like Indian Chicken Curry (page 95).

---

1 cup fat-free plain Greek yogurt

½ medium cucumber, peeled, seeded, and minced

2 tablespoons finely chopped whole scallions

1 tablespoon finely chopped fresh mint leaves

1 tablespoon finely chopped fresh cilantro leaves

1 teaspoon freshly squeezed lemon juice

⅛ teaspoon sea salt

In a medium resealable plastic container, mix the yogurt, cucumber, scallions, mint, cilantro, lemon juice, and salt. Cover and refrigerate for at least 1 hour.

Makes 12 (2-tablespoon) servings

Per serving: 13 calories, 2 g protein, 1 g carbohydrates (trace sugar), trace fat, 0 g saturated fat, 0 mg cholesterol, < 1 g fiber, 25 mg sodium

INDIAN CHICKEN CURRY

This dish is spicy (as many traditional Indian curries are), so you may want to save this recipe for an adult-only occasion. Also note that this dish is higher in sodium than most others in this book, because I really wanted to create an authentic taste. Many curry dishes at Indian restaurants contain as much as 4,499 milligrams of sodium per serving, so this still has a fraction of the salt of any curry you'll find on a restaurant menu.

1¼ pounds trimmed boneless, skinless chicken breasts, cut into 1½" pieces

1 teaspoon avocado oil

2 tablespoons salt-free Indian seasoning blend or rub (I used The Spice Hunter Salt Free Curry Seasoning Blend), divided

¾ teaspoon salt, or more to taste, divided

Olive oil spray (propellant free)

¾ cup coarsely chopped sweet onion

2 teaspoons freshly minced garlic

1 can (15 ounces) all-natural no-salt-added diced tomatoes

¾ cup light coconut milk

2 tablespoons chopped cilantro leaves, divided

Add the chicken to a large bowl and drizzle with the oil. Sprinkle 1 tablespoon of the seasoning and ¼ teaspoon of the salt over the chicken and toss well, until the chicken pieces are evenly coated.

Place a large nonstick soup pot or saucepan with a lid over medium-high heat. When hot, add half of the chicken. Cook for 2 to 3 minutes per side, or until the chicken pieces are browned. Remove the chicken to a plate or bowl. Add the remaining chicken, repeating the cooking process, and remove the browned chicken to the plate or bowl. Mist the pot with spray and place it back over the heat. Add the onion and garlic and cook, stirring frequently, for 1 to 2 minutes, or until the onions begin to soften. Add the chicken back to the pot, followed by the tomatoes with their juice, coconut milk, 1 tablespoon of the cilantro, and the remaining 1 tablespoon spice rub and ½ teaspoon salt. Stir well to combine. Bring the mixture to a simmer, then reduce the heat to medium-low. Cover the pan and cook, stirring occasionally, for 30 minutes, or until the chicken is very tender. Stir in the remaining 1 tablespoon cilantro and season with salt, if desired. Serve immediately.

Makes 4 (heaping 1-cup) servings

Per serving: 238 calories, 34 g protein, 9 g carbohydrates (1 g sugar), 6 g fat, 3 g saturated fat, 82 mg cholesterol, 2 g fiber, 553 mg sodium

SIONE FA'S LU PUAKA (LEAVES WITH PORK)

Sione Fa of Season 7 says that this dish is traditionally made by smoking pork underground, and then wrapping the pork in taro leaves and smothering the whole thing in mayonnaise. Here Sione offers a much lighter version that still gives you the wonderful flavor of smoked pork with a fraction of the fat and calories. It's a great dish for a cold winter's night.

1¼ pounds pork tenderloin, cut into 1½" cubes

1 teaspoon olive oil

½ teaspoon all-natural hickory-flavored liquid smoke (I used Wright's All-Natural Hickory Seasoning Liquid Smoke)

Sea salt, to taste

Ground black pepper, to taste

1 bag (6 ounces) baby spinach leaves

1 medium sweet onion, chopped

½ cup light coconut milk

You will need to have a roasting (for the oven) or grilling plank. Preheat the grill to high, or set the oven to the temperature as directed in the plank instructions.

Add the pork to a medium mixing bowl. Drizzle the oil and liquid smoke over top and season with salt and pepper. Toss until well coated.

Follow the package directions for your plank (most grill planks require soaking prior to grilling; most oven planks need to be warmed in the oven prior to adding your food). Place the cubes of meat side by side on the plank (it's okay if they are touching). Cook them until no longer pink (my oven roasting plank took 20 to 25 minutes on 350°F).

Meanwhile, cut a piece of nonstick foil about 2 feet long and fit it into an 8" x 8" baking dish, so that it is lined and two sides stand above the pan (you will be creating a sealed pocket in the end). Repeat that with a second piece of foil so the long sides stand in the opposite direction. Lay half of the spinach leaves in the bottom of the dish.

When the pork comes out of the oven (if using the oven instead of the grill), change the oven temperature to 400°F. Otherwise, preheat the oven to 400°F.

Top the spinach leaves with the cooked pork, followed by the onion and then the other half of the spinach leaves. Pour the coconut milk over the top, then seal the pocket by bringing the tops of the foil halves together and folding them down, then folding in the sides, being sure that it is completely sealed. Roast for 45 minutes, or until the pork is so tender that it comes apart with a fork.

Note: Be very careful when opening the pouch and be sure to use an oven mitt. The steam will be very hot. After opening the pouch, season with salt and pepper, to taste, and serve immediately.

Makes 4 (1¼-cup) servings

Per serving: 221 calories, 32 g protein, 9 g carbohydrates (4 g sugar), 6 g fat, 3 g saturated fat, 92 mg cholesterol, 2 g fiber, 119 mg sodium

Rulon Gardner

Each day when you exercise, pay attention to how your body feels. You'll start to notice that your body has learned how to work better, and you'll see the results. Look in the mirror and see what you want to be, then make it happen.

CHICKEN SATAY

You can serve this satay as an appetizer or as a filling main dish with a side salad. Be sure to serve the dipping sauce in tiny bowls. A tablespoon of sauce is actually more than you'd think, but if you serve it in a ramekin or a larger bowl, it won't look like much. It's amazing how, when served correctly, healthy food can be elegant.

- 2 tablespoons all-natural lower-sodium soy sauce
- 2 tablespoons all-natural rice wine
- 2 tablespoons freshly squeezed lime juice
- 2 tablespoons coconut sugar
- 2 tablespoons freshly minced garlic
- 2 tablespoons minced peeled fresh ginger
- 2 tablespoons minced shallots
- 1 tablespoon toasted (or roasted) sesame oil
- 1 teaspoon all-natural salt-free curry powder
- 1 pound trimmed boneless, skinless chicken breasts, pounded to ⅓" thickness and cut into 16 relatively equal strips across the breasts
- 4 tablespoons Asian Peanut Sauce (page 207)

To a large resealable plastic bag, add the soy sauce, rice wine, lime juice, sugar, garlic, ginger, shallots, oil, and curry powder. Seal the bag and shake it until the ingredients are well combined. Open the bag, add the chicken strips, and reseal the bag, removing any excess air. Make sure the chicken is well coated. Let it marinate in the refrigerator for at least 6 hours or overnight.

Soak 16 (6" to 10") wooden skewers in water for at least 30 minutes (or have metal skewers ready). Preheat a grill to high heat.

Remove one chicken strip from the bag and thread it onto a skewer by weaving it so that it is secured in at least two spots down the center of the piece of chicken. Repeat until all of the chicken strips are secured on skewers. Place the skewers side by side on the grill so they do not touch. Grill them for 2 to 3 minutes per side, or until the chicken is no longer pink inside. Serve immediately with the peanut sauce.

Makes 4 servings

Per serving (4 skewers + 1 tablespoon of sauce): **222 calories, 28 g protein, 9 g carbohydrates (5 g sugar), 7 g fat, 1 g saturated fat, 66 mg cholesterol, <1 g fiber, 323 mg sodium**

Mexican Makeovers

Who doesn't have a weakness for Mexican food? If you've spent any time in Mexico, chances are you found some wonderfully fresh, healthy options, full of fruits and vegetables, whole grains, and proteins. But at most Mexican restaurants north of the border, you're more likely to find giant portions of deep-fried fare smothered in a mound of cheese and sour cream.

You're much better off preparing Mexican food at home, where you can control the preparation method and steer clear of added calories. *Biggest Loser* Club nutrition expert Greg Hottinger, RD, says, "I love making burritos by loading up a whole wheat tortilla with veggies, grilled chicken or black beans, and a spoonful of guacamole. I skip the cheese and top it off with salsa. Yum! It satisfies my taste for Mexican food, and I'm eating a healthy meal."

When Season 10's Jessica Delfs returned home to Tucson, Arizona, after her time on *The Biggest Loser* Ranch, she struggled to avoid the taco trucks that she says are "everywhere." She dealt with her cravings by creating healthier versions of the dishes she loves—and she shared her creations with us.

"Some great recipes I adapted come from pollo asado street tacos and pollo asado carmelos, which is basically two corn tortillas with grilled chicken and cheese melted in the middle," Jessica said. "All of these recipes are super simple and basically use the same ingredients you'll find in the tacos from those street trucks, with a fraction of the calories."

Whether you're craving a burrito, a taco, nachos, or a quesadilla, you'll be sure to find a recipe in this chapter that will make you say "Olé!"

SMOKY BREAKFAST QUESADILLA

I've noticed that the contestants often eat a lot of salsa with their meals—I mean, why not? It really is the perfect low-calorie condiment. But I've also seen many of them grow tired of the same flavors. This quesadilla was inspired by one contestant who said she "just couldn't handle one more dish with salsa on top!" I suggested she try one of the many other varieties of salsa available and brought her a jar of the smokier version used in this recipe. She was instantly hooked.

Olive oil spray (propellant free)

¼ cup red onion strips

¼ cup green or red bell pepper strips

1 (8") whole spelt tortilla or other all-natural, low-fat, whole grain tortilla (I used Rudi's Organic Bakery Whole Spelt Tortillas)

1 ounce (about ⅓ cup) finely shredded all-natural, low-fat Cheddar cheese (I used Cabot 75% Reduced Fat Cheddar)

4 large egg whites

2 tablespoons fresh fire-roasted salsa

Lightly mist a small nonstick skillet with spray and place it over medium heat. Add the onion and pepper. Cook, stirring occasionally, for 6 to 9 minutes, or until they are crisp-tender and lightly browned on the outside.

Meanwhile, place a nonstick frying pan, large enough for a tortilla to lie flat, over medium-low heat. Put the tortilla in the pan. Sprinkle on the cheese evenly, covering the tortilla. Let the cheese melt.

When the onions and peppers are cooked, transfer to a bowl and cover to keep warm. Mist the skillet again with spray and add the egg whites. As they begin to set, use a wooden spoon to scrape from one side of the pan to the other, to "scramble" them. Continue scrambling until no runny egg remains. Then spoon the eggs over the cheese on one half of the tortilla. Sprinkle the onion-pepper mixture over that. When the cheese is melted, fold the bare half over the filled half.

Transfer the quesadilla to a serving plate and cut into 4 wedges. Top with the salsa. Serve immediately.

Makes 1 serving

Per serving: 293 calories, 29 g protein, 35 g carbohydrates (5 g sugar), 6 g fat, 3 g saturated fat, 10 mg cholesterol, 3 g fiber, 642 mg sodium

BREAKFAST TACOS

I always thought that tortillas were made simply from corn, water, and salt. So imagine my surprise when I realized that all of the packaged tortillas at my local grocery store contained a laundry list of artificial ingredients. Be sure to read the labels when buying tortillas, and choose the most natural ones you can find.

While this dish may seem a little higher in fat than some of the others in this book, much of the fat content comes from the addition of heart-healthy avocado. You can reduce the amount of avocado or omit it, if you are trying to cut down on the fat in your diet.

Olive oil spray (propellant free)

4 large egg whites

¼ –½ teaspoon all-natural salt-free Mexican or Southwest seasoning (I used Mrs. Dash Southwest Chipotle)

2 (about 6") preservative-free yellow corn tortillas

½ ounce (5 tablespoons) finely shredded, all-natural, low-fat Cheddar (I used Cabot 75% Reduced Fat Cheddar)

2 tablespoons well-drained pico de gallo or fresh salsa

½ cup finely shredded romaine lettuce leaves

⅙ avocado, pit removed and sliced thin

All-natural hot sauce, to taste (I used Cholula), optional

Lightly mist a small microwave-safe bowl with spray. Add the egg whites and seasoning and microwave for 30 seconds on high. Continue microwaving in 30-second intervals until the eggs are just a bit runny on top. Then, using a fork, stir them to break into large "scrambled" pieces. By the time you scramble and stir them, the residual heat should have cooked away the runniness. If they are still undercooked, cook them in 10-second intervals until just done. Leave the bowl in the microwave until you're ready to plate the dish.

Place a small nonstick skillet over medium-high heat. When hot, add the tortillas, one at a time. When they're warm on one side, flip them. When both sides are warm, transfer each to a large serving plate. Divide the scrambled egg whites evenly over the center one-third of each tortilla. Top the eggs with the cheese, followed by the pico de gallo. Top each taco evenly with the lettuce and avocado slices. Serve immediately with hot sauce, if desired.

Makes 1 serving

Per serving: **253 calories, 22 g protein, 26 g carbohydrates (1 g sugar), 8 g fat, 1 g saturated fat, 5 mg cholesterol, 5 g fiber, 353 mg sodium**

CARNE ASADA

This steak cooks very, very quickly. Be sure to watch it carefully so that you don't overcook it. One full minute per side on my grill resulted in a well-done steak when I used two ½-pound pieces.

It's really important that you tent meat after cooking it. Simply place a piece of foil over and around the meat, without actually sealing the foil, so steam can easily escape. This allows the juices to redistribute. If you cut into the steak the second it comes off the grill, you'll lose all of its natural juices.

---

2 teaspoons unsweetened cocoa powder

1½ teaspoons chili powder

1½ teaspoons chipotle chile pepper (the one in a jar in the spice aisle)

1½ teaspoons smoked paprika

¼ teaspoon salt

18 ounces trimmed top round steak, preferably grass fed (see note)

1 teaspoon olive oil

In a small bowl, mix the cocoa powder, chili powder, chipotle chile pepper, paprika, and salt until well combined.

Place the steak on a clean, flat work surface. Using the toothed side of a meat mallet, tenderize the steak by pounding both sides to a ⅛" thickness (it can have some small holes in it but shouldn't be so flat it tears apart). Rub the oil over all of the steak, then rub the seasoning mixture evenly over that. Allow the steak to stand for 15 to 20 minutes.

Meanwhile, preheat a grill to high heat. When hot, grill the steak for 45 seconds to 1 minute per side for medium-rare. Transfer to a plate and tent with foil (place the foil loosely over the top) for 10 minutes. Cut across the grain into thin slices and serve immediately.

Makes 4 (4-ounce) servings

Note: *Always make sure your meat is trimmed of all visible fat.*

Per serving: 145 calories, 28 g protein, 2 g carbohydrates (trace sugar), 6 g fat, 2 g saturated fat, 56 mg cholesterol, 1 g fiber, 227 mg sodium

FIESTA FISH TACOS

When you buy your fish, always be sure to ask for "the thicker end." The closer the meat is to the tail, the tougher it tends to be since the tail does most of the work to make the fish swim. Here you particularly want a nice thick piece of fish to ensure that your tacos will be meaty.

---

4 ounces halibut filet, preferably wild-caught, cut into 8 relatively equal pieces

1 teaspoon salt-free Southwest or Mexican seasoning

Sea salt, to taste (optional)

Olive oil spray (propellant free)

2 (about 6") preservative-free yellow corn tortillas

1 tablespoon Fish Taco Sauce (page 209)

½ cup finely shredded cabbage

1 tablespoon chopped fresh cilantro leaves

¼ cup well-drained fresh pico de gallo or fresh salsa

2 small lime wedges

Place the fish in a small bowl and sprinkle it with seasoning and salt, if desired. Toss well to coat.

Place a small nonstick skillet over medium-high heat. When it's hot, lightly mist it with spray and add the fish. Cook, turning occasionally, for 3 to 5 minutes, or until the pieces are browned on the outsides and flake easily in the center. Remove from the pan and place in a bowl. Cover to keep warm.

Place the tortillas one at a time in another small nonstick skillet over medium heat to warm them. When warm on one side, flip them. When both sides are warm, transfer each to a dinner plate. Spread ½ tablespoon of the sauce evenly down the center of each tortilla. Divide the fish evenly among the tortillas, followed by the cabbage, cilantro, and salsa. Serve immediately, with lime wedges on the side.

Makes 1 serving

Per serving: 275 calories, 26 g protein, 27 g carbohydrates (1 g sugar), 7 g fat, trace saturated fat, 36 mg cholesterol, 3 g fiber, 207 mg sodium

JESSICA DELFS' POLLO ASADO FLAUTAS

I recommend adding either a couple of pinches of salt to the outside of the tortillas just before cooking—if you dip your fingers in water and run them along the tortillas just before broiling, salt will stick—or add a couple of pinches to the chicken. That said, if you can't find organic tortillas, or you choose not to use them, you won't need to add any salt.

½ teaspoon chili powder

½ teaspoon garlic powder

½ teaspoon smoked paprika

½ teaspoon ground black pepper

Sea salt, to taste

4 ounces trimmed boneless, skinless chicken breasts

4 (about 6") preservative-free yellow corn tortillas (Jessica uses Whole Foods 365 brand)

Olive oil spray (propellant free)

1 ounce (⅓ cup) finely shredded, all-natural, low-fat Cheddar (I used Cabot 75% Reduced Fat Cheddar)

½ cup all-natural fresh salsa

½ cup finely shredded cabbage

Place an oven rack in the center position in the oven. Preheat the broiler. Line a small baking sheet with foil. Preheat a grill to high heat.

In a small bowl, mix the chili powder, garlic powder, paprika, pepper, and salt. Rub it evenly over both sides of the chicken. Grill the chicken for 3 to 5 minutes per side, or until no longer pink inside. Place the chicken on a plate and loosely tent it with foil.

Place the tortillas between 2 slightly damp paper towels and microwave on high for 10 to 15 seconds, or just long enough to make them pliable.

Slice the chicken into thin strips across the breasts (not lengthwise). Place one-quarter of the chicken strips down the middle of each tortilla and roll tightly, securing each with a toothpick.

Lightly mist each flauta (chicken roll) with spray on both sides and place them side by side on the prepared baking sheet so they do not touch. Broil, watching them closely to assure they do not burn, for 2 to 4 minutes. Gently flip them and broil them for 1 to 3 minutes longer, or until golden brown and crisp throughout.

Remove the toothpicks (they should stay wrapped at this point) and divide them between 2 serving plates. Top each flauta with 1½ tablespoons of cheese, 2 tablespoons of salsa, and 2 tablespoons of shredded cabbage. Serve immediately.

Makes 2 servings

Per serving: **217 calories, 20 g protein, 25 g carbohydrates (<1 g sugar), 5 g fat, <1 g saturated fat, 38 mg cholesterol, 3 g fiber, 188 mg sodium**

Trainer Tip: Cara Castronuova

Drink a large glass of water before eating a meal. It will help prevent you from overeating.

SHRIMP OPEN BURRITO

One of the keys to successful healthy eating is to be sure to keep your meals balanced. You always want about 4 ounces of lean protein per meal, along with plenty of veggies. Here I've created an open burrito, because using a tortilla large enough to completely enclose enough meat (protein) and fillings to create an entire meal would add too many calories and carbs. So instead of skimping on the protein, I like to make "open wraps." This open burrito tastes as delicious as a "closed" one, can be picked up like a burrito, and is quick and easy to make.

4 ounces peeled raw shrimp (51–60 count or larger), preferably wild-caught

1 teaspoon salt-free Mexican or Southwest seasoning

Olive oil spray (propellant free)

1 (8") whole spelt tortilla or other all-natural, low-fat, whole grain tortilla (I used Rudi's Organic Bakery Whole Spelt Tortillas)

2 teaspoons all-natural low-fat sour cream

¾ ounce finely shredded, all-natural, low-fat Cheddar (I used Cabot 75% Reduced Fat Cheddar)

¼ cup shredded romaine lettuce

⅓ cup drained all-natural fresh salsa

Cholula or other all-natural hot sauce, to taste (optional)

In a medium bowl, toss the shrimp in the seasoning until evenly coated.

Place a small nonstick skillet over medium-high heat. When hot, lightly mist it with spray and add the shrimp. Cook, stirring occasionally, for 3 to 5 minutes, or until the outsides are browned and the insides are cooked through.

Meanwhile, place a medium nonstick skillet over medium heat. Place the tortilla in the skillet for 30 seconds to 1 minute per side until just warmed. Transfer the warmed tortilla to a plate. Starting from the 12 o'clock position (as if the tortilla were a clock), spread the sour cream over a strip that is 3" wide and stretches about 4" down to the center of the tortilla. Top that with the cheese, followed by the lettuce, salsa, and shrimp. Drizzle the hot sauce over top, if desired. Fold the sides at the 3 o'clock and 9 o'clock positions into the center over the filling, then fold up the bottom (6 o'clock) and serve.

Makes 1 serving

Per serving: **335 calories, 35 g protein, 35 g carbohydrates (3 g sugar), 8 g fat, 3 g saturated fat, 183 mg cholesterol, 2 g fiber, 569 mg sodium**

CHORIZO NACHOS

I served these nachos at the reunion dinner I hosted for former Biggest Loser contestants before the Season 10 finale, and they were a huge hit. This dish is one of the favorite recipes among everyone in my test kitchen as well. These nachos would be very impressive to serve on game day—what could be more perfect for snacking than cheesy nachos with homemade chorizo? Since you can make the chorizo in advance, you can whip up these nachos in no time.

Olive oil spray (propellant free)

2½ ounces uncooked Homemade Chorizo (page 206)

1 ounce (about 11 chips) all-natural baked tortilla chips

⅓ cup rinsed and drained canned, no-salt-added black beans, heated

2 tablespoons all-natural salsa con queso, heated

¼ cup well-drained fresh pico de gallo or fresh salsa

1 tablespoon finely chopped whole scallions

Place a small nonstick skillet over medium-high heat. When hot, lightly mist the pan with spray and add the chorizo. Cook, breaking it into large chunks, for 1 to 2 minutes, or until no longer pink.

Arrange the chips on a dinner plate. Top them evenly with the beans, then the chorizo. Drizzle the salsa con queso evenly over top. Top them with the pico de gallo and scallions and serve immediately.

Makes 1 serving

Per serving: 335 calories, 22 g protein, 47 g carbohydrates (<1 g sugar), 7 g fat, 1 g saturated fat, 37 mg cholesterol, 7 g fiber, 557 mg sodium

HOMEMADE CHORIZO SAUSAGE LINKS

I'm a huge fan of making my own sausage, because I can create the flavor I love while keeping it as healthy as possible. Not only is this chorizo delicious when crumbled in omelets and on Chorizo Nachos (page 115), it's also an amazing accompaniment to any Mexican favorite when prepared as links.

Olive oil spray (propellant free)

1 recipe uncooked Homemade Chorizo (page 206)

Preheat the oven to 400°F. Line a small nonstick baking sheet with parchment paper and mist it lightly with spray.

Divide the chorizo mix into 8 equal portions (about a heaping ¼ cup each). Shape each into a log about 4½" long and an even thickness. Place the logs side by side, not touching, on the prepared baking sheet. Mist them lightly with spray. Bake for 9 to 11 minutes, or until completely cooked through.

Makes 8 servings

Per serving (1 link): **101 calories, 14 g protein, 5 g carbohydrates (trace sugar), 3 g fat, <1 g saturated fat, 37 mg cholesterol, 2 g fiber, 221 mg sodium**

Courtney Crozier

I came to *The Biggest Loser* Ranch knowing that I could lose weight—I had lost more than 100 pounds on my own, but I've learned that this whole journey is so much more than just losing weight. I've learned to embrace change in all aspects of my life—physically, mentally, and emotionally. You have to change your mind before you can make true changes. The transformation will happen from the inside out.

SPINACH MUSHROOM QUESADILLA

You'll be surprised by how decadent and cheesy this quesadilla tastes, especially if you use the Cabot's Cheddar as recommended. Just make sure not to overcook the spinach—you want to cook it until it's just wilted. If you cook it too long, the spinach leaves will shrivel and take on a burnt flavor.

Olive oil spray (propellant free)

1 cup sliced button mushrooms

½ teaspoon all-natural, no-salt-added fajita or other Mexican seasoning (I used The Spice Hunter Salt Free Fajita Seasoning Blend)

Sea salt, to taste

½ cup packed chopped baby spinach leaves

1 (8") whole spelt tortilla or other all-natural, low-fat, whole grain tortilla (I used Rudi's Organic Bakery Whole Spelt Tortillas)

1¼ ounces (scant ½ cup) finely shredded all-natural, low-fat Cheddar (I used Cabot's 75% Reduced Fat Cheddar)

Place a medium nonstick skillet over medium-high heat. When hot, lightly mist the pan with spray and add the mushrooms. Sprinkle them with the fajita seasoning and salt. Cook, stirring occasionally, for 5 to 7 minutes, or until the mushrooms are tender and most of the liquid has evaporated. Stir in the spinach leaves and cook for 30 seconds to 1 minute longer, or until the spinach is soft and wilted. Remove the pan from the heat.

Place a nonstick skillet, large enough for the tortilla to lay flat, over medium heat. Lay the tortilla in the pan. After 30 seconds, flip the tortilla and cover it evenly with the cheese. Then spoon the mushroom-spinach mixture evenly over one-half of the cheese. Fold the tortilla in half so that the side without the filling covers the side with the filling. Cook the quesadilla for 2 to 4 minutes, or until it just starts to brown in spots. Then flip it and cook for 2 to 4 minutes longer, or until the second side is just starting to brown a bit in spots and the cheese is melted through.

Cut the quesadilla into 4 equal wedges as if you are cutting pizza slices. Serve immediately.

Makes 1 serving

Per serving: 242 calories, 19 g protein, 31 g carbohydrates (4 g sugar), 7 g fat, 3 g saturated fat, 13 mg cholesterol, 3 g fiber, 469 mg sodium

Regional American Classics

Just as every country around the world offers a unique culinary experience of distinctive flavors, so is our country a melting pot of regional cuisines. From the tropics of Hawaii to the swamps of the deep South, the streets of Philadelphia to the deserts of the Southwest, virtually every town in the United States cooks up a signature dish that its residents just can't live without.

Chef Devin says that when she started writing this chapter, she intended to cover the hometown favorites in every region of the country. But she admitted that the flavorful traditions of the South soon began to take center stage. That's probably because these much-loved dishes—such as fried chicken, sweet potato casserole, and blackened catfish—are typically not foods that you can enjoy when you're trying to lose weight. So Devin set out to overhaul these American classics so that anyone could enjoy them.

Louisiana natives Brady and Vicky Vilcan of Season 6 have a passion for living a healthy lifestyle and for the spicy foods of Cajun country. They've contributed two of their favorites to this chapter, both of which rely on what they refer to as "the holy trinity" of Cajun ingredients: onions, bell peppers, and celery.

The state of Pennsylvania is represented with dishes from the east and west sides of the region: Philly Buffalo Cheese Steak (page 151) and Pittsburgh Steak (page 153). In both cases, what is typically a greasy, high-fat tradition has been re-created using buffalo sirloin, a healthy protein that contains only 2 grams of fat per 4-ounce serving.

So turn the page and see if your local favorite is represented in this chapter. And if your regional cuisine didn't make it into the book, mosey on across state lines and try some of your neighbor's best dishes. There's nothing like home cooking.

VICKY AND BRADY VILCAN'S FIERY CHICKEN & SAUSAGE GUMBO

Vicky said you can place the flour in a cast-iron skillet and put it in the oven at 350°F until it browns slightly, instead of browning it on the stove top, if that's easier. She suggests serving the gumbo over brown rice, which is a great option. It's also delicious served over whole wheat pasta.

½ cup whole wheat pastry flour

12 ounces nitrate-free lean chicken or turkey sausage, cut into thin slices on a diagonal (I used Applegate Organics Andouille Chicken & Turkey Sausage)

1 pound trimmed boneless, skinless chicken breasts, cut into cubes

4 cups all-natural low-sodium chicken broth

Olive oil spray (propellant free)

4 cups water

1 cup chopped white or yellow onion

1 cup chopped green bell pepper

1 cup chopped celery

3 tablespoons salt-free Cajun or Creole seasoning, or to taste (I used The Spice Hunter Salt Free Cajun Creole Seasoning Blend)

1 bunch whole scallions, chopped (about 1 cup)

2 teaspoons salt-free gumbo filé (I used The Spice Hunter Salt Free Gumbo Filé Blend)

Place a large nonstick soup pot over medium heat. Add the flour. Stir it frequently until it browns lightly (Vicky says to be sure that you stir it often or it will burn, but don't stir it constantly it or will take a very long time to toast). Remove it from the pot and set aside.

Turn the heat to medium-high. Add the sausage and cook, stirring occasionally, for 2 to 3 minutes, or until it's just browned. Transfer it to a medium bowl.

Meanwhile, put the broth and water in another large pot and bring to a boil.

Return the pot that contained the sausage to the heat. Mist it with spray and add the chicken in a single layer. Cook the chicken for 1 to 2 minutes per side, or until browned on both sides. Add it to the sausage mixture.

Respray the soup pot and place it over medium heat. Add the onion, bell pepper, and celery. Cook, stirring occasionally, for 6 to 9 minutes, or until the onions are clear. Stir in a few tablespoons at a time of the toasted flour until it is well mixed. Pour the boiling broth and water into the mixture (if the water is not boiling, the flour will clump). Add the Cajun seasoning and bring the liquid to a boil. Then turn the heat to medium-low and simmer for 20 minutes. Add the cooked sausage and chicken and simmer for 30 minutes longer. Turn off the heat. Add the scallions and filé and stir well to combine. Let it sit with the lid on for 10 minutes. Ladle into 6 serving bowls and serve immediately.

Makes 6 (1¹⁄₂-cup) servings

Per serving: **260 calories, 30 g protein, 18 g carbohydrates (4 g sugar), 6 g fat, 2 g saturated fat, 84 mg cholesterol, 4 g fiber, 532 mg sodium**

Trainer Tip: Bob Harper

In the kitchen, it's about portion control. Read labels and know exactly what you are putting in your body. We need those bodies running like fine-tuned machines. If you get a little protein, some carbs, and a little fat, you've had a good meal!

NEW ORLEANS–INSPIRED BLACKENED CATFISH

You might have seen (or even used) blackened seasoning from the grocery store. Blackening meat or fish by seasoning it with a special spice blend, then searing the outsides, is a popular technique in Cajun and Creole cooking. Many commercially available blackened seasonings contains a ton of sodium, so I prefer to make my own in order to control the amount of salt used.

1 tablespoon dried thyme

1 teaspoon freshly ground black pepper

1 teaspoon garlic powder

½ teaspoon ground red pepper, or more to taste

¼ teaspoon sea salt

1 pound catfish fillets, cut into 4 equal pieces (see note)

2 teaspoons all-natural unsalted butter, melted

Mix the thyme, black pepper, garlic powder, red pepper, and salt in a small bowl until well combined.

Place the fish fillets side by side on a sheet of waxed paper or parchment paper. Brush lightly on both sides with the butter, then sprinkle on the seasoning mixture. Gently rub the seasoning into the fillets.

Place a large nonstick skillet over medium-high heat. When hot, add the fish, side by side. Cook for 1 to 2 minutes per side, or until golden brown. Turn the heat to medium and continue cooking for 2 to 4 minutes, or until they are cooked through (the fish should flake easily). Transfer the fillets to a serving platter or place on 4 dinner plates. Serve immediately.

Makes 4 servings

Note: *In an ideal world, you would buy either four 4-ounce catfish fillets or two 8-ounce fillets to cut in half. But that might not be possible. If you end up with odd-size fillets, the cooking time will likely be different.*

Per serving: 132 calories, 19 g protein, 1 g carbohydrates (trace sugar), 5 g fat, 2 g saturated fat, 71 mg cholesterol, <1 g fiber, 196 mg sodium

PULLED CHICKEN SANDWICH

Anyone who hails from a region of our country that knows its barbecue is familiar with the much-loved classic pulled-pork sandwich. This pulled chicken version is leaner but just as delicious.

You may find it odd that I suggest shredding the chicken with a pastry blender. Before I tried it, I would have agreed. But it's amazing how much more quickly the chicken shredded using my pastry blender, so I'm now hooked. It's a great shortcut, if you happen to have this handy kitchen tool. If not, just use forks or your fingers.

1   tablespoon whole grain oat flour

¼   teaspoon garlic powder

⅛   teaspoon salt

    Pinch ground black pepper

1   pound trimmed boneless, skinless chicken breasts, cut into 1½" cubes

½   tablespoon extra-virgin olive oil

⅔   cup orange juice (not from concentrate)

⅔   cup distilled white vinegar

2   tablespoons all-natural hickory-flavored liquid smoke (I used Wright's All-Natural Hickory Seasoning Liquid Smoke)

4   tablespoons all-natural, no-sugar-added barbecue sauce (I used OrganicVille Original BBQ Sauce)

    Olive oil spray (propellant free)

1   cup white or yellow onion strips

4   all-natural, whole grain English muffins (I used Rudi's Organic Bakery Whole Grain Wheat English Muffins)

In a medium plastic bag, combine the flour, garlic, salt, and pepper. Add the chicken and shake the bag until the chicken is coated. Refrigerate the chicken for at least 15 minutes.

Preheat a large nonstick soup pot or saucepan over medium-high heat. When it's hot, add the oil, then the chicken. Brown the chicken for 1 minute per side, then turn the heat to medium and add the orange juice, vinegar, and liquid smoke. Bring it to a boil, then reduce the heat to low (the liquid should still be boiling slightly). Cover and cook the chicken, stirring occasionally, for 30 to 40 minutes, or until very tender. (The liquid will absorb into the meat, and the pieces should be so tender they fall apart when poked with a wooden spoon.) Using a slotted spoon, transfer the chicken (along with a bit of the liquid) to a medium mixing bowl. Using your fingers, 2 forks, or a pastry blender, separate the pieces until the chicken is shredded.

Discard the extra liquid in the pot. Return the shredded chicken to the pot and place it over medium heat. Stir in 2 tablespoons of the barbecue sauce. Continue stirring until the mixture is hot.

Meanwhile, during the last 5 minutes of cooking, mist a small nonstick frying pan with spray and place it over medium heat. Add the onion and cook for 5 minutes, or until tender.

Place the muffin halves, cut sides down, in a large nonstick frying pan over medium heat (work in batches if necessary). Cook for 3 to 5 minutes, or until just toasted. Place each muffin bottom on a plate. Pile one-quarter of the chicken mixture onto each. Top each one-quarter of the onions and drizzle with ½ tablespoon of the remaining barbecue sauce. Add the muffin tops. Serve immediately.

Makes 4 servings

Per serving: **328 calories, 32 g protein, 38 g carbohydrates (11 g sugar), 5 g fat, <1 g saturated fat, 66 mg cholesterol, 4 g fiber, 486 mg sodium**

Hannah Curlee

I have learned that there is only one *me*. I am worth all of the hard work, and it's okay to shed a few tears or even some buckets of tears as I go through this process. I am still learning to be the best Hannah I can be and letting myself seek and accept change.

CHICKEN-"FRIED" STEAK

It's essential to pound the meat and allow it to soak in buttermilk before cooking it. That way, even a lean cut of meat like top round will still be tender like fattier cuts traditionally used in this dish.

---

1 pound trimmed top round steak, preferably grass fed

1 cup low-fat buttermilk

¾ cup all-natural whole wheat panko-style bread crumbs

1 teaspoon garlic powder

¾ teaspoon freshly ground black pepper, plus more to taste

½ teaspoon paprika

¼ teaspoon ground turmeric

⅛ teaspoon salt

2 pinches ground red pepper

Olive oil spray (propellant free)

Place the steak on a clean, flat work surface. Using the toothed side of a meat mallet, pound it on both sides, until it is ¼" thick. Cut it into 4 equal pieces. Place the pieces in a medium plastic bag and pour the buttermilk over them. Marinate in the refrigerator for at least 6 hours or overnight.

Place 2 sheets of waxed paper or parchment paper on a clean, flat work surface.

Add the panko to the bowl of a food processor fitted with a chopping blade. Process until they are fine crumbs. Spoon the bread crumbs onto a plate.

In a small bowl, mix the garlic powder, black pepper, paprika, turmeric, salt, and red pepper.

Remove 1 steak from the buttermilk and let any excess drip off. Over a sheet of waxed paper, sprinkle both sides of the steak evenly with about one-quarter of the spice mixture. Immediately transfer the steak to the crumbs. Coat both sides. Then place the breaded steak on the second sheet of waxed paper. Repeat with the remaining steaks, placing them side by side so they don't touch on the paper. Mist the tops of both sides of the steaks with spray and sprinkle with additional pepper to taste.

(continued)

Place a large nonstick skillet over medium-high heat. When hot, mist it with spray. Cook the steaks for 1 to 3 minutes per side, or until the breading is crisp on the outside and the insides are cooked to desired doneness (be careful not to overcook the steaks—if you do, the breading will become soggy and fall off the steaks). Lightly mist the finished steaks with spray and serve immediately.

Makes 4 servings

Per serving: 166 calories, 27 g protein, 11 g carbohydrates (1 g sugar), 4 g fat, 2 g saturated fat, 51 mg cholesterol, 2 g fiber, 159 mg sodium

Jesse Wornum

Get clear about what you want to accomplish. Plan what you want to do and how you'll do it, then do it. If your plan isn't successful the first time, regroup and restart.

VICKY VILCAN'S DIRTY RICE

This traditional Cajun dish got its name from the browned chicken livers or giblets that are typically used to make it. Though this rice may not have the same "dirty" appearance as traditional recipes, Vicky feels her version still captures the classic Cajun flavor.

---

3 cups cooked brown rice

1 pound extra-lean ground turkey (I used Jennie-O)

2 teaspoons salt-free Cajun or Creole seasoning, or to taste (I used The Spice Hunter Salt Free Cajun Creole Seasoning Blend)

¼ teaspoon + ⅛ teaspoon salt

Olive oil spray (propellant free)

1 cup chopped sweet onion

1 cup chopped celery

1 cup chopped green bell pepper

1 tablespoon freshly minced garlic

1 cup all-natural low-sodium chicken broth

½ cup chopped fresh parsley leaves

½ cup finely chopped whole scallions

1 tablespoon all-natural hot sauce, or more to taste (I used Tabasco)

In a medium bowl, add the turkey, Cajun seasoning, and ¼ teaspoon salt. With a fork or clean hands, mix until well combined.

Place a large nonstick skillet over medium-high heat. When hot, lightly mist with spray and add the turkey. Cook the turkey, breaking it into large chunks as you do, for 5 to 7 minutes, or until lightly browned and no longer pink. Remove to a plate or bowl and set aside.

Mist the pan again with spray and place it back over medium-high heat. Add the onion, celery, and bell pepper. Cook the mixture, stirring occasionally, for 3 to 6 minutes, or until the vegetables are tender and lightly browned. Add the garlic and broth. Bring the mixture to a simmer and cook for 2 to 4 minutes, or until some of the liquid has evaporated. Return the turkey to the pan and add the rice. Cook for 1 minute, or until most of the liquid has evaporated. Add the parsley and scallions and cook for 2 to 3 minutes longer.

(continued)

Drizzle the hot sauce over the rice mixture and stir well to combine. Remove the pan from the heat and cover. Let sit for 10 minutes. Stir in the remaining ⅛ teaspoon salt. Divide among 4 serving bowls and serve immediately.

Makes 4 servings

Per serving: 334 calories, 33 g protein, 49 g carbohydrates (4 g sugar), 3 g fat, trace saturated fat, 45 mg cholesterol, 6 g fiber, 356 mg sodium

Marci Crozier

My best fitness tip is to cross-train. Don't do the same thing over and over. Shake it up! Interval training is great, and working out in groups can be very motivating and add accountability to your routine.

GARLIC SOUTHERN FRIED CHICKEN

I particularly like the garlic flavor of this chicken, though feel free to use your favorite salt-free seasoning (such as Cajun) if you're not a huge fan of garlic. To achieve an even crisper, oven "fried" crust, cook the chicken on the bottom rack of your oven.

---

4 small bone-in chicken breasts (approximately 7 to 8 ounces each), trimmed of skin and visible fat (see note)

1¼ cups low-fat buttermilk

Olive oil spray (propellant free)

2 teaspoons all-natural salt-free garlic herb seasoning or your favorite all-natural salt-free seasoning (I used Spice Hunter Salt Free Garlic Herb Bread Blend)

½ teaspoon salt, plus more to taste, if desired

1 cup all-natural whole wheat panko-style bread crumbs

Add the chicken breasts and buttermilk to a large resealable plastic bag or container. Rotate the breasts so they are completely coated, then seal the bag or container. Marinate them in the refrigerator at least 6 hours or overnight, rotating them once or twice.

Preheat the oven to 450°F. Lightly mist a medium nonstick baking sheet with spray.

In a small bowl, mix the seasoning and salt.

Add the panko to a medium shallow bowl.

Remove 1 chicken breast from the buttermilk. Let any excess buttermilk drip off it, then sprinkle the entire breast (both sides) evenly with about one-quarter of the seasoning mixture. Dip the chicken in the panko, rotating it to cover completely. Place the breaded chicken breast face down (ribs up) on the prepared pan. Repeat with the remaining breasts, arranging them on the baking sheet so they do not touch.

Lightly mist the chicken with spray. Bake for 10 minutes, then gently flip the breasts, being careful not to remove any breading. Lightly

(continued)

mist them again with spray and continue to bake for 12 to 15 minutes longer, or until the breading is crispy and the chicken is no longer pink inside. Sprinkle with additional salt, if desired. Serve immediately or refrigerate for up to 2 days to eat cold.

Makes 4 servings

Note: *If you have trouble finding small chicken breasts, look for the larger chicken breasts halves that are about 1 pound each (I've found these are generally easier to find). Ask your butcher to remove the skin and cut them in half, leaving you with 4 approximately 8-ounce breast pieces.*

Per serving: **176 calories, 25 g protein, 14 g carbohydrates (1 g sugar), 2 g fat, trace saturated fat, 55 mg cholesterol, 2 g fiber, 393 mg sodium**

COLLARD GREENS WITH BACON & SWEET ONION CONFETTI

When working with collard greens, use only the leaves and thin stems. The ribs and the coarse stems should be thrown away. You should keep this in mind when you buy your greens, since a lot of the weight will be discarded once you remove the stems.

Olive oil spray (propellant free)

4 ounces (about 4 strips) 94% lean or leaner nitrate-free peppered turkey bacon (I used Wellshire Classic Sliced Turkey Peppered Bacon), cut into small pieces

1½ cups coarsely chopped sweet onion

1 tablespoon freshly minced garlic

⅔ cup all-natural low-sodium chicken broth

2 tablespoons cider vinegar

2 tablespoons coconut sugar

½ teaspoon crushed red pepper flakes, or more to taste

1½ pounds coarsely chopped collard green leaves

Sea salt, to taste

Ground black pepper, to taste

Lightly mist a large nonstick soup pot with spray and place it over medium-high heat. Add the bacon, onion, and garlic. Cook for 2 to 4 minutes, or until the onions are tender and the bacon begins to brown slightly. Remove half of the mixture from the pan and set it aside to cool (see note on page 137).

To the remaining bacon mixture, add the broth, vinegar, sugar, pepper flakes, and one-half of the collard greens. Toss until the greens are wilted enough to fit the remaining collard greens in the pot. Add the remaining greens and toss until well combined. Cover the pot and turn the heat to medium-low. Simmer, stirring about every 15 minutes, for 30 to 40 minutes, or until the greens are very tender.

Just before the collard greens are finished, place a small nonstick skillet over medium heat. Mist it with spray and add the remaining bacon mixture. Reheat it, stirring occasionally until hot.

(continued)

Use a slotted spoon to transfer the collard green mixture to a serving bowl or 4 individual bowls, letting any excess liquid remain in the pot. Top the bowls evenly with the remaining bacon and onion mixture and additional pepper flakes, if desired. Season to taste with salt and pepper.

Makes 4 (1¾-cup) servings

Note: *It is best to cover and refrigerate the bacon mixture after it cools before reheating it.*

Per serving: **145 calories, 11 g protein, 22 g carbohydrates (8 g sugar), 2 g fat, trace saturated fat, 20 mg cholesterol, 7 g fiber, 242 mg sodium**

Trainer Tip: Brett Hoebel

Goals are like road maps: The more specific, the faster you reach your destination. Setting a goal is key to getting results, but it's important to set SMART goals (specific, measurable, attainable, realistic, and time-bound). Instead of setting a goal like "I'm going to lose weight," set a goal like "I'm going to lose 5 pounds in one month."

AMY PARHAM'S "FRIED" OKRA

Amy Parham of Season 6 uses the same method for making this okra to cook breaded green tomatoes and squash. She said she often serves the tomatoes with all-natural roasted red pepper hummus for dipping, instead of a creamy dip. In my test kitchen, we love dipping the okra in all-natural low-fat ranch dressing (such as Follow Your Heart Low Fat Ranch Dressing, which has 25 calories and 1.5 grams of fat per 2-tablespoon serving).

Olive oil spray (propellant free)

1 large egg white

1 teaspoon fat-free milk

3 tablespoons whole grain cornmeal (I used Arrowhead Mills Organic Yellow Corn Meal)

1 teaspoon salt-free Cajun seasoning (I used The Spice Hunter Salt Free Cajun Creole Seasoning Blend)

⅛ teaspoon salt

6 medium okra pods, rinsed and dried (about 2¼ ounces total)

Preheat the oven to 350°F. Place a sheet of parchment paper over a small baking sheet. Lightly mist it with spray.

In a medium shallow bowl, whisk together the egg white and milk until the mixture bubbles slightly.

In another medium shallow bowl, stir together the cornmeal, Cajun seasoning, and salt until well combined.

Dip a piece of okra into the egg wash until it is completely coated. Let any excess drip off (remove any "globs" of egg white from the okra), then transfer the okra to the bowl with the cornmeal mixture. Roll the okra in the cornmeal mixture, sprinkling it over the okra to coat evenly, until completely breaded. Place it on the prepared baking sheet. Repeat with the remaining pieces of okra, placing them side by side so they do not touch on the baking sheet.

Lightly mist the tops with spray. Bake, flipping halfway through and respraying the tops after you flip them, for 14 to 16 minutes per side, or until the okra is tender and the crumbs are crisp and golden brown.

Makes 1 serving

Per serving: 72 calories, 4 g protein, 13 g carbohydrates (1 g sugar), 1 g fat, trace saturated fat, trace cholesterol, 3 g fiber, 181 mg sodium

MINI CITRUSY SWEET POTATO CASSEROLES

I find the citrus flavor of these little casseroles very craveable. I like using fresh lemon and orange zest to brighten the taste of the sweet potatoes. A quick tip: Zest the citrus first, then juice it. You'll find it much easier to zest the fruit before it's cut in half.

1½ pounds sweet potatoes, peeled and cut into 1½" cubes (see note)

Olive oil spray (propellant free)

¼ cup 100% orange juice (not from concentrate)

2 tablespoons fat-free evaporated milk

1 tablespoon freshly squeezed lemon juice

1 tablespoon all-natural unsalted butter, melted

1 tablespoon light agave nectar

1 teaspoon lemon zest

1 teaspoon orange zest

½ teaspoon pumpkin pie spice, or more to taste

⅛ teaspoon salt

Ground black pepper, to taste

2 tablespoons finely chopped pecans

Add the sweet potatoes to a large pot of cold, lightly salted water and place it over high heat. When it comes to a boil, cook for 12 to 15 minutes, or until very tender.

Preheat the oven to 375°F. Lightly mist six 3½" (approximately ½-cup capacity) ramekins with spray.

Drain the potatoes and add them to a medium mixing bowl along with the orange juice, evaporated milk, lemon juice, butter, agave, zests, pumpkin pie spice, and salt. With a hand mixer, beat the mixture until smooth. Season with pepper.

Divide the mixture evenly among the prepared ramekins. Sprinkle the pecans evenly on top. Bake for 12 to 15 minutes, or until the potatoes are hot throughout and the nuts are lightly toasted. Let stand 5 minutes and serve.

Makes 6 servings

Note: *Be sure to cut the potatoes into relatively uniform pieces so they cook evenly.*

Per serving: 114 calories, 2 g protein, 19 g carbohydrates (7 g sugar), 4 g fat, 1 g saturated fat, 5 mg cholesterol, 2 g fiber, 94 mg sodium

HAWAIIAN POKE

If you've ever vacationed in Hawaii, you've probably eaten poke. It's a traditional Hawaiian dish similar to tuna tartare, but the tuna tends to be cubed, not chopped. There are many variations of poke, but I decided to go the more authentic route and create a basic version. Remember that any time you consume raw fish, you should always buy the best, freshest fish you can find.

---

8 ounces sushi-grade ahi tuna, cut into ¾" cubes

Pinch sea salt

¼ cup 2" long sweet onion slivers

½ teaspoon minced fresh jalapeño pepper, or more to taste (wear plastic gloves when handling)

1 tablespoon + 1 teaspoon all-natural lower-sodium soy sauce

1 teaspoon toasted sesame oil

Mix the tuna and sea salt in a medium resealable plastic container. Add the onion and jalapeños. Drizzle the soy sauce and sesame oil over top and toss gently until well combined. Cover and refrigerate for 1 to 2 hours. Divide the tuna between 2 martini glasses or small, decorative serving bowls and serve immediately.

Makes 2 servings

Per serving: 158 calories, 27 g protein, 3 g carbohydrates (<1 g sugar), 3 g fat, <1 g saturated fat, 52 mg cholesterol, trace fiber, 328 mg sodium

HAWAIIAN GRILLED CHICKEN BREAST SANDWICH

If you want to call this sandwich one of your "splurge" meals, you can add more teriyaki sauce. The teriyaki flavor in this recipe is subtle, but the grilled pineapple gives it a wonderful burst of sweetness. Each additional tablespoon of the sauce has about 20 calories, 2.5 grams of sugar, and 180 milligrams of sodium.

4 ounces trimmed boneless, skinless chicken breast

1½ tablespoons all-natural lower-sodium teriyaki sauce (I used Simply Boulder Culinary Sauces Truly Teriyaki), see note

1 ½"-thick slice fresh pineapple

1 all-natural low-fat, whole grain English muffin (I used Rudi's Organic Bakery Whole Grain Wheat English Muffins)

½ leaf green leaf lettuce

⅛ cup red onion slivers, or to taste

Place the chicken breast on a cutting board and lay a sheet of waxed paper over it. Using the flat head of a meat mallet, pound the chicken breast, working from the center out, until it is about ½" thick throughout.

Brush ½ tablespoon of the sauce over the chicken and coat it on all sides. Place the chicken in a bowl, cover with plastic wrap, and let stand for 10 minutes.

Preheat a grill to high. Grill the chicken for 3 to 5 minutes per side, or until it is no longer pink inside. Meanwhile, grill the pineapple for 1 to 2 minutes per side, or until it's warmed through, has grill marks, and is slightly tender. About 1 minute before the chicken breast is done, place the English muffin halves, cut sides down, on the grill to toast lightly.

Place the bottom half of the muffin, toasted side up, on a plate. Add the lettuce, onion, then the chicken breast and the pineapple. Spoon the remaining 1 tablespoon of teriyaki sauce over the top and place the other half of the muffin on top. Serve immediately.

Makes 1 serving

Note: *Be sure to read the labels to find the best available option. Look for teriyaki sauce that's sweetened with agave nectar or honey.*

Per serving: 312 calories, 32 g protein, 36 g carbohydrates (12 g sugar), 4 g fat, trace saturated fat, 66 mg cholesterol, 4 g fiber, 551 mg sodium

MARYLAND CRAB CAKES

If you don't have a good nonstick baking sheet, line your baking sheet with nonstick foil to prevent the cakes from sticking. Please note that the crab cakes are very delicate, so handle them carefully to avoid any crumbling.

Olive oil spray (propellant free)

1 pound jumbo lump crabmeat, drained if necessary

2 tablespoons freshly squeezed lemon juice

1 cup all-natural whole wheat panko-style bread crumbs

2 tablespoons finely chopped dill leaves, divided

2 tablespoons finely chopped tarragon leaves, divided

¼ cup minced shallots

3 tablespoons all natural reduced-fat sandwich spread (I used NatureNaise Organic Spread Original with Sunflower Oil)

2 teaspoons all-natural prepared horseradish

¼ teaspoon ground red pepper

2 ounces finely shredded low-fat almond mozzarella cheese (I use Lisanatti)

Preheat the oven to 450°F. Lightly mist a medium nonstick baking sheet with spray.

In a small mixing bowl, gently mix the crab with the lemon juice, being careful to keep the lumps of crab intact as much as possible.

Put the panko in a small resealable plastic bag and seal it, removing all the air from the bag. Using the flat side of a meat mallet, pound the panko into fine crumbs. Transfer the crumbs to a medium shallow bowl. Mix in 1 tablespoon of the dill and 1 tablespoon of the tarragon.

In a second small mixing bowl, whisk the shallots, sandwich spread, horseradish, red pepper, and the remaining 1 tablespoon dill and 1 tablespoon tarragon until well combined. Using a spatula, gently mix in the crab and the cheese, again being careful to keep the meat in lumps (don't shred it).

(continued)

Divide the mixture into 8 equal portions. Form one into a mound that is 2" in diameter across the top. Carefully roll it in the panko to cover the crab cake and place it on the prepared baking sheet. Repeat with the remaining cakes and panko (some panko will remain), placing them on the baking sheet side by side so they do not touch. Place the baking sheet in the freezer for 10 minutes (this helps the cakes keep their shape).

Lightly mist the tops with spray. Bake the cakes for 12 to 14 minutes, or until the breading is crisp and they are hot through (see note). Serve immediately.

Makes 4 (2-cake) servings

Note: *If the cakes lose shape in the oven, gently use a spatula to reshape them as soon as they are removed from the oven. Then let them rest for 3 minutes before serving.*

Per serving: **209 calories, 27 g protein, 15 g carbohydrates (<1 g sugar), 4 g fat, 1 g saturated fat, 88 mg cholesterol, 2 g fiber, 531 mg sodium**

TOSSED CALIFORNIA COBB

The most common lunch eaten by the team in my kitchen is a big salad. We love chopping up piles of lean proteins, veggies, and herbs. This salad has quickly become a go-to, in part because it's very filling, but also because it packs many of our favorite ingredients.

Throughout the book, I reference "loosely packed" lettuces, herbs, etc. What I mean by this is that you shouldn't just let the items fall into the measuring cup and you shouldn't jam them in there either. You want to gently tuck them in, so to speak.

2½ cups loosely packed shredded Romaine lettuce leaves

2 cups loosely packed shredded fresh baby spinach leaves

3 ounces Essential Grilled Chicken (page 205), cut into ½" cubes

2 chopped hard-boiled egg whites

½ ounce (½ slice) cooked, finely chopped, lean, nitrate-free turkey bacon (I used Applegate Hardwood Smoked Uncured Turkey Bacon)

½ cup seeded, finely chopped tomatoes

3 tablespoons finely chopped avocado

3 tablespoons all-natural reduced-fat, lower-sodium yogurt-based chunky blue cheese dressing (I used Bolthouse Farms Creamy Yogurt Chunky Blue Cheese Dressing)

To a medium mixing bowl, add the lettuce, spinach, chicken, egg whites, bacon, tomatoes, and avocado. Drizzle the dressing over the top and toss the mixture until well combined. Transfer it to a plate and serve immediately.

Makes 1 serving

Per serving: 314 calories, 36 g protein, 14 g carbohydrates (6 g sugar), 14 g fat, 3 g saturated fat, 77 mg cholesterol, 7 g fiber, 541 mg sodium

PHILLY BUFFALO CHEESE STEAK

I've heard a lot of folks proudly say, "I had a buffalo burger," when asked if they had a healthy lunch. And while buffalo (also known as bison) can be a great option, just like all meat, the cut makes all the difference in the world. Look for sirloin—a 4-ounce serving is leaner than beef or even pork, weighing in at only 2 grams of fat per serving.

6" piece all-natural whole wheat baguette

4 ounces trimmed bison sirloin (see note on page 152)

Olive oil spray (propellant free)

¼ cup onion slivers

¾ ounce light provolone cheese (I used Sargento)

2 teaspoons all-natural sliced, pickled hot chile peppers, or to taste, optional

1 tablespoon all-natural low-sodium, no-sugar-added ketchup

Cut the baguette in half (but not all the way through) to open it for a sandwich. Weigh the baguette. If it weighs more than 2 ounces, pull out enough of the inside of the bread to make it 2 ounces.

Shave the steak by holding a very sharp knife at a 45-degree angle and cutting slivers from the steak, basically tearing it until it's all shaved. It should be cut much more finely than if it were simply sliced.

Place a medium nonstick skillet over medium-high heat and mist it with spray. Add the onion. Cook, stirring frequently, for 4 to 7 minutes, or until tender. Remove from the pan and cover to keep warm.

Turn the heat to high and add the bison shavings. Pull apart the shavings using 2 wooden spoons or spatulas to ensure even browning as the shavings cook. Don't overstir the meat or it won't brown at all. Cook for 2 minutes, or until the steak is just barely pink on the inside and lightly browned on the outside. Pile it toward one side of the pan and turn the heat down to medium. Place the cheese over the pile of

(continued)

meat. Add the open baguette, cut side down, to the empty side of the pan and toast until it's a light golden brown. Open the baguette on a plate.

When the cheese is melted, use a spatula to transfer the meat to the baguette. Top with the onions and chile peppers, if desired, followed by the ketchup.

Makes 1 serving

Note: *Using a larger bison steak, and then measuring 4 ounces of shavings, makes it easier to shave the steak. Shaving the steak is the key to this sandwich actually being "Philly style."*

Per serving: 354 calories, 35 g protein, 33 g carbohydrates (4 g sugar), 8 g fat, 3 g saturated fat, 92 mg cholesterol, 3 g fiber, 454 mg sodium

Arthur Wornum

No matter how hard a workout gets, just remember that it always comes to an end. So soldier through it. You can do anything that you set your mind to.

PITTSBURGH STEAK

Pittsburgh is known for its die-hard sports team loyalty as well as some not-so-healthy indulgences. I have to admit, I was pretty shocked when I first learned that it's a regional tradition for Steelers fans (that's meant to be inclusive of all residents of Pittsburgh) to actually put french fries on salads and in sandwiches! The town is also known for serving steaks that are charred on the outside and pretty much raw on the inside—just like this one, except that this one is made with an extremely lean cut of beef.

½ teaspoon avocado oil

8 ounces trimmed London broil, preferably grass fed, cut into 2 equal steaks

Sea salt, to taste

Ground black pepper, to taste

Garlic powder, to taste

2 tablespoons all-natural no-sugar-added steak sauce (I used Whole Foods 365 Organic Steak Sauce)

Place an oven rack in the top position. Preheat the broiler. Line a small metal baking sheet with nonstick foil.

Rub the oil over the steaks, followed the salt, pepper, and garlic powder. Place the steaks side by side on the baking sheet so they do not touch. Broil them for 1 to 2 minutes per side, or just until they are charred on the outside (they should be rare inside). Remove from the oven and tent the steaks with foil for 5 minutes. Serve immediately with steak sauce.

Makes 2 servings

Per serving: **180 calories, 24 g protein, 3 g carbohydrates (2 g sugar), 7 g fat, 2 g saturated fat, 37 mg cholesterol, 0 g fiber, 272 mg sodium**

7

Mediterranean Flavor

The Mediterranean diet is often touted as one of the healthiest in the world. After all, with a near-perfect climate, the region offers some of the world's freshest, most sought-after ingredients and, as a culture, places an emphasis on eating small portions of high-quality ingredients. But one of those healthy ingredients—the one that's used liberally in almost every Mediterranean dish—must be used with some restraint when you're watching your calories: olive oil.

"So many people hear that olive oil is healthy," says Greg Hottinger, RD, nutrition expert for *The Biggest Loser* Club. "And while it is a source of heart-healthy fat, most don't realize that each tablespoon contains 120 calories—and ¼ cup, which is easy to consume with your bread, has 480 calories. If you ate only an extra tablespoon of olive oil every day, you'd gain 12 pounds in a year."

The key to using olive oil sparingly is to invest in a mister, so that you can spray a small amount on your pans

or your finished food as needed. Chef Devin also suggests that you buy olive oil and then pour it into your mister, because many canned olive oil sprays contain propellants and other additives.

Another ingredient key to Mediterranean cooking is often used to balance olive oil: lemon juice. Lemon trees grow throughout the Mediterranean region, and their juices and skin are often utilized in both sweet and savory dishes. Devin uses fresh lemon juice in her Greek Salad (page 158) to really make the flavors pop. In fact, she recommends adding fresh lemon juice to just about any dish that needs a little extra burst of bright, fresh flavor. For example, she says that the Mediterranean Tabbouleh Salad (on the opposite page) can be taken to a whole other level with just a sprinkle of this one simple ingredient.

From the Greek Isles to the Middle East, you'll find a wide array of mouthwatering dishes from this popular culinary region. Bring the flavors of the Mediterranean into your very own kitchen!

Trainer Tip: Jillian Michaels

After a big meal, instead of taking a nap or watching TV, take a walk instead. A 45-minute walk after a big meal can enhance your metabolism by as much as 15 percent.

MEDITERRANEAN TABBOULEH SALAD

This tasty and nutritious salad, compliments of the very talented Chef Cameron Payne of The Biggest Loser *Resort, can be made in advance and stored for a couple days in your refrigerator. It's a great salad to pack for weekday lunches—especially if you throw some Essential Grilled Chicken (page 205) or grilled salmon or shrimp on top. If you love the flavor of fresh lemon as much as I do, feel free to squeeze on a little extra juice. For me, it makes this salad even more delicious and super craveable!*

---

2 cups water

1 cup uncooked bulgur wheat (look for it in the cereal aisle)

½ cup chopped fresh parsley leaves

½ cup seeded and chopped tomatoes

½ cup seeded, diced cucumbers

⅛ cup chopped fresh mint leaves

⅛ cup freshly squeezed lemon juice, or more to taste

¼ teaspoon salt, or to taste

¼ teaspoon ground black pepper, or to taste

In a medium nonstick saucepan, bring the water to a boil. Add the bulgur. Reduce the heat and simmer, covered, for 15 minutes, or until the water has absorbed. Spread the bulgur evenly over a baking sheet and refrigerate it for 10 minutes to cool.

Meanwhile, in a medium mixing bowl, combine the parsley, tomatoes, cucumbers, mint, lemon juice, salt, and pepper. Add the cooled bulgur and stir until well combined. Serve immediately, or refrigerate and allow the flavors to meld.

Makes 4 (generous 1-cup) servings

Per serving: 132 calories, 5 g protein, 30 g carbohydrates (1 g sugar), <1 g fat, trace saturated fat, 0 mg cholesterol, 7 g fiber, 158 mg sodium

For more ways to live *The Biggest Loser* lifestyle, go to biggestloser.com.

GREEK SALAD

Greek salads are, by far, one of my personal favorites. If I had my druthers, when I order them in restaurants, I'd eat every single delicious bite of feta and even ask for extra olives. But, alas, both ingredients are insanely high in sodium, so I can't. In order to add as much cheese and as many olives as possible, I've opted to skip using a bottled dressing (most have at least a couple hundred milligrams of sodium per tablespoon). Instead, I used plenty of fresh lemon juice to create a dressing that bursts with flavor, making this salad one of my at-home favorites.

---

2   tablespoons freshly squeezed lemon juice, or more to taste

1   teaspoon freshly minced garlic, or more to taste

1   teaspoon extra-virgin olive oil

1   cup ¾" cubes cucumber

1   cup 1" cubes red bell pepper

1   cup 1" cubes Roma tomato

6   kalamata olives, cut in half lengthwise

1   ounce all-natural light feta cheese, cut into ⅛" cubes

4   ounces Essential Grilled Chicken (page 205), cut into slices

½   teaspoon dried mint leaves

In a small resealable plastic container, shake together the lemon juice, garlic, and oil to make the dressing.

In a large bowl, toss the cucumbers, peppers, tomatoes, olives, cheese, and the dressing. Transfer the salad to a large serving plate. Top it with the chicken and then the mint, crushing the leaves slightly with your fingers as you sprinkle it over the salad. Serve immediately.

Makes 1 serving

Per serving: 346 calories, 35 g protein, 26 g carbohydrates (13 g sugar), 12 g fat, 4 g saturated fat, 71 mg cholesterol, 6 g fiber, 863 mg sodium

BACON-WRAPPED FIGS

When you buy goat cheese, you'll often see both the cheese log and crumbled varieties. Either is fine to use for this recipe, but if you use the crumbles, be extra careful to pack the crumbles into the teaspoon measure. You're not using a lot of cheese here, so you want to make sure you don't skimp on the full teaspoon the recipe allows.

Olive oil spray (propellant-free)

4 medium (about 1¼ ounces total) dried figs

1 slice (about 1 ounce) 94% fat-free or leaner, nitrate-free turkey bacon (I used Applegate Hardwood Smoked Uncured Turkey Bacon)

1 teaspoon goat cheese, packed

Preheat the oven to 325°F. Line a small baking sheet with foil. Lightly mist the foil with spray.

Fill a nonstick medium saucepan, with a tight-fitting lid, half full with water. Place it over high heat and bring the water to a boil. Add the figs, remove the pan from the heat, and cover. Let the figs stand for 5 minutes, then drain. Allow them to cool slightly before handling.

Meanwhile, slice the bacon in half crosswise. Slice each piece in half lengthwise, leaving 4 equal strips.

Place the figs on a cutting board. Using a sharp knife, cut a 1" opening lengthwise down the middle of each fig. Stuff each fig with ¼ teaspoon of the cheese, then wrap a strip of bacon around the widest part of each fig. Secure the bacon with a toothpick, then place the wrapped figs on the prepared baking sheet. Bake for 10 to 12 minutes, or until they are warmed through. Serve immediately.

Makes 1 serving

Per serving: **136 calories, 8 g protein, 22 g carbohydrates (16 g sugar), 3 g fat, < 1 g saturated fat, 28 mg cholesterol, 3 g fiber, 224 mg sodium**

SPANAKOPITA BITES

I love cocktail parties—it's fun to get dressed up, and there's always the chance of meeting new, interesting people (and trying delicious food)! Thank goodness I'm aware that, on average, even a few of the tiny little hors d'oeuvres contain as many calories as a meal. For instance, four pieces of traditional spanakopita have about 280 calories, 7 grams of protein, 16 grams of carbohydrates, 21 grams of fat, and 499 milligrams of sodium. Notice the difference between those and five pieces of these delectable little gems. Once you try these, you'll swear off the originals forever!

2 whole scallions, trimmed and cut into thirds

2 medium cloves fresh garlic

1½ cups loosely packed fresh flat-leaf parsley

1 bag (12 ounces) frozen chopped spinach, defrosted

2 ounces (about ½ cup) crumbled light feta cheese

1 large egg white

⅛ teaspoon salt

  Pinch ground nutmeg

20 all-natural whole wheat mini phyllo shells (see note)

Preheat the oven to 450°F. Place the phyllo shells side by side on a small baking sheet.

Add the scallions, garlic, and parsley to the bowl of a food processor fitted with a chopping blade. Process until finely chopped, stopping to scrape down the sides of the bowl, if needed. Transfer the mixture to a medium mixing bowl and set aside.

Place the spinach in a fine strainer and squeeze as much moisture from it as possible. Then transfer the spinach to a clean, lint-free dish towel and squeeze it until all of the water is removed (if moisture remains, the filling will not be rich). Add the spinach to the onion mixture along with the feta, egg white, salt, and nutmeg. Mix until well combined.

Divide the mixture among the phyllo shells, forming it into tight balls, then placing them so they are neatly mounded over and lightly packed in the shells. Bake them for 8 to 10 minutes, or until the shells are a light golden brown and the filling is hot. Serve immediately.

Makes 20 bites

Note: *Be sure to check the ingredient list on packaged phyllo to make sure it's made from whole wheat flour.*

Per serving (5 bites): 143 calories, 8 g protein, 18 g carbohydrates (2 g sugar), 3 g fat, <1 saturated fat, 3 mg cholesterol, 2 g fiber, 443 mg sodium

CHAR-GRILLED BABA GHANNOUJ WITH PITA CHIPS

This isn't exactly the same as traditional baba ghannouj, though I feel it captures all of the wonderful flavors and velvety texture of the real thing. I like to leave the skin on the eggplant for extra flavor and nutrition. For an even leaner snack, enjoy it with carrot or celery sticks instead of the whole grain pita chips.

1 pound eggplant, unpeeled, top trimmed, cut into ¾"-thick slices

Olive oil spray (propellant-free)

Salt, to taste

Ground black pepper, to taste

1 medium clove garlic

¼ cup all-natural fat-free plain Greek yogurt

2 tablespoons chopped fresh flat-leaf parsley

1½ tablespoons all-natural well-stirred tahini

1½ tablespoons freshly squeezed lemon juice

Ground red pepper to taste (optional)

4 ounces all-natural low-fat, whole grain pita chips (I used Whole Foods 365 Everyday Value Whole Wheat Pita Chips with Flax & Onion)

Preheat a grill to high heat.

Lightly mist both sides of the eggplant slices with spray. Season them with salt and pepper. Grill for 4 to 6 minutes per side, or until the eggplant is very soft and has dark grill marks.

Coarsely chop the eggplant and transfer it to the bowl of a mini food processor fitted with a chopping blade. Add the garlic, yogurt, parsley, tahini, and lemon juice. Pulse for 1 minute, or until the mixture is mostly smooth, stopping to scrape down the sides of the bowl if necessary. Season with additional salt and red pepper, if desired. Serve immediately, with the pita chips.

Makes 4 servings

Per serving (heaping ⅓ cup + 1 ounce pita chips): **183 calories, 8 g protein, 27 g carbohydrates (4 g sugar), 6 g fat, trace saturated fat, 0 mg cholesterol, 7 g fiber, 231 mg sodium**

LAMB KEBABS

Sumac is a tangy spice made from the blossoms of the rhus plant. The flowers are dried and ground into a deep reddish/purple powder that is commonly used in Middle Eastern cooking. I find it has a lemony, almost salty flavor. I love using it in marinades for various meats, or sprinkling it on top of hummus or Greek salads. It's very inexpensive, and I can usually find it in the ethnic foods aisle at my local grocery store. If you don't see it there, you can easily order it online.

⅔ cup fat-free plain yogurt

2 tablespoons + 1 teaspoon freshly minced garlic

1 tablespoon + 1 teaspoon red wine vinegar

1 tablespoon + 1 teaspoon sumac

1½ teaspoons extra-virgin olive oil, divided

1 teaspoon salt

1 pound trimmed top round lamb, cut into 16 large cubes (about 2" x 2" each)

20 cherry tomatoes

20 sweet onion squares, about 1½"

In a medium bowl, stir together the yogurt, 2 tablespoons garlic, the vinegar, 1 tablespoon sumac, 1 teaspoon of the oil, and the salt until well combined. Add the lamb to a large resealable freezer bag. Pour the marinade over the meat. Marinate for 24 hours.

Soak 4 (at least 12") wooden skewers in water for at least 30 minutes (or have metal skewers ready). Preheat a grill to high.

Add the tomatoes, onion, and the remaining ½ teaspoon olive oil, 1 teaspoon garlic, and 1 teaspoon sumac to a medium mixing bowl. Toss until combined.

Onto one skewer, thread a tomato, a piece of onion, and a piece of lamb, then tomato, onion, lamb, tomato, onion, lamb, tomato, onion, lamb, tomato, and onion. Repeat with the remaining skewers, veggies, and lamb until you have 4 kebabs. Grill for 45 seconds to 1 minute and 15 seconds per side for medium rare. Serve immediately, or keep warm until serving.

Makes 4 servings

Per serving: 222 calories, 27 g protein, 10 g carbohydrates (5 g sugar), 9 g fat, 3 g saturated fat, 71 mg cholesterol, 2 g fiber, 492 mg sodium

8

A European Tour

When we asked Chef Devin about her favorite recipes in this chapter, her voice turned dreamy as she confessed that the Placki Kartoflane (Polish Potato Pancakes) pull her back in over and over "like an ocean current."

"Typically, these are served in Polish households with sour cream or applesauce," she said, "but these are so good, I just sprinkled them with a tiny bit of sea salt. The onions already give them a lot of rich flavor. Truly, out of all the recipes in this book, this is the one where I had to restrain myself. I kept wanting to go back and eat more!"

In addition to Eastern European favorites like the potato pancakes (page 185) and Ground Turkey Cabbage Rolls (page 181)—courtesy of Season 3's Jen Eisenbarth, a midwesterner of German heritage—you'll also find recipes from some of Europe's most celebrated (and sinful) food cultures, including France. But Chef Devin shows us that any recipe can be adjusted for a healthy lifestyle—even the decadently rich Steak au Poivre (page 178), which is usually topped with a creamy, buttery sauce that probably contains as many calories as the steak itself! Chef Devin's dish tastes just as velvety and delicious, but contains only 6 grams of fat.

In this chapter, you'll discover how to make the kinds of dishes you can usually only find on the menus at white-tablecloth restaurants. We even have some waistline-friendly versions of favorite dishes from the culinary world's new hotspot, Spain. The recipes will help you save calories and money, and are perfect dishes for dinner parties or other special occasions. Impress your guests with a sophisticated European menu!

GAZPACHO ANDALUZ

Last year, I had the pleasure of spending some time at The Biggest Loser *Resort and got to sample Chef Cameron Payne's delicious, healthy meals. Needless to say, I was very happy when he kindly agreed to share his gazpacho recipe for this book. It's a great warm weather soup since it's served chilled and requires no cooking whatsoever. Plus with only 61 calories a cup, how can you go wrong?*

6 medium cloves garlic

4 cups teardrop or grape tomatoes

1 medium cucumber, peeled and cut into large pieces

1 medium red bell pepper, cored, seeded, and cut into large pieces

½ medium yellow onion, cut into large pieces

2 tablespoons balsamic vinegar

½ teaspoon sea salt, or to taste

¼ teaspoon ground black pepper, or to taste

Add the garlic, tomatoes, cucumber, bell pepper, and onion to the bowl of a food processor fitted with a chopping blade. Process until relatively smooth. Pour the mixture into a medium resealable container. Stir in the vinegar, salt, and pepper. Refrigerate for at least 30 minutes. Season to taste with additional salt and pepper, if desired. Serve chilled.

Makes 4 (1¼-cup) servings

Per serving: 61 calories, 3 g protein, 13 g carbohydrates (8 g sugar), < 1 g fat, trace saturated fat, 0 mg cholesterol, 4 g fiber, 213 mg sodium

For more ways to live *The Biggest Loser* lifestyle, go to biggestloser.com.

CHAMPIÑONES AL AJILLO (MUSHROOMS WITH GARLIC)

This super low-cal dish makes a perfect first course or can be served as a side dish alongside chicken, pork, or any other healthy protein. A Spanish restaurant staple, it's also a great dish to serve at a tapas party.

Olive oil spray (propellant free)

8 ounces crimini or button mushrooms, quartered

2 tablespoons all-natural low-sodium vegetable broth

1 tablespoon dry sherry

1 tablespoon freshly minced garlic

½ tablespoon freshly squeezed lemon juice

½ tablespoon finely chopped fresh flat-leaf parsley

Sea salt, to taste

Ground black pepper, to taste

Place a large nonstick skillet over medium-high heat. When hot, mist the pan with spray and add the mushrooms. Cook, stirring occasionally, for 4 to 6 minutes, or until most of the liquid has evaporated and the mushrooms are tender.

Add the broth, sherry, garlic, and lemon juice. Bring to a boil, then reduce the heat to medium. Continue cooking for 2 to 3 minutes longer, or until the mushrooms are very tender and the liquid is reduced. Remove the pan from the heat and stir in the parsley. Season with salt and pepper. Divide the mixture between 2 small serving bowls and serve immediately.

Makes 2 servings

Per serving: **46 calories, 3 g protein, 6 g carbohydrates (2 g sugar), trace fat, trace saturated fat, 0 mg cholesterol, <1 g fiber, 17 mg sodium**

GAMBAS AL AJILLO (SHRIMP WITH GARLIC)

You'll notice throughout the book I often specify "freshly squeezed lemon juice" and "freshly minced garlic." So often, people buy bottled lemon juice and minced garlic that's been jarred with oil and citric acid. Not only are these processed ingredients not as good for you, but they also don't taste as good as the real thing. Since this is such a simple recipe, using the best quality ingredients makes a big difference in the overall flavor of the dish.

1¼ pounds jumbo (21 to 25 count) peeled and deveined shrimp, tails left on

1 teaspoon avocado olive oil

Sea salt, to taste

Ground black pepper, to taste

¼ cup freshly squeezed lemon juice

2 tablespoons dry sherry

2 tablespoons freshly minced garlic

1 teaspoon paprika

⅛ teaspoon crushed red pepper flakes, or more to taste

2 tablespoons finely chopped fresh flat-leaf parsley

Toss the shrimp with the oil in a large bowl. Season with salt and pepper.

Place a large nonstick skillet over high heat. When hot, add half of the shrimp and cook for 1 to 2 minutes per side, or until the shrimp are pink and mostly cooked through. Remove the shrimp to a plate or bowl. Place the pan back over the heat and repeat with the remaining shrimp.

Add the cooked shrimp back to the pan. Add the lemon juice, sherry, garlic, paprika, and pepper flakes. Cook, stirring often, for 1 to 3 minutes, or until the shrimp are completely cooked and the liquid has reduced slightly. Remove the pan from the heat and stir in the parsley. Transfer the shrimp and sauce to a large serving bowl. Serve immediately.

Makes 4 (¾-cup) servings

Per serving: 197 calories, 29 g protein, 11 g carbohydrates (2 g sugar), 4 g fat, < 1 g saturated fat, 215 mg cholesterol, 1 g fiber, 303 mg sodium

MINI QUICHE LORRAINES

If you don't have a 3¾" cookie cutter, don't worry. You can use the rim of an empty 3¾"-diameter can to cut the tortillas or even simply cut 3¾" circles using a butter knife. If you don't have a really great nonstick muffin tin, cut pieces of parchment along with your tortilla circles. Place one under each tortilla circle as you press it into the pan.

Olive oil spray (propellant free)

½ cup (about ½ small) finely chopped sweet onion

2 ounces (about 2 slices) nitrate-free turkey bacon (I used Applegate Hardwood Smoked Uncured Turkey Bacon), cut into ¼" squares

6 large egg whites

⅓ cup fat-free milk

2 teaspoons Dijon mustard

Ground black pepper, to taste

4 (8") whole spelt tortilla or other all-natural, low-fat, whole grain tortilla (I used Rudi's Organic Bakery Whole Spelt Tortillas)

2 ounces (about ¾ cup) finely shredded all-natural, low-fat Cheddar cheese (I used Cabot 75% Reduced Fat Cheddar)

Preheat the oven to 375°F. Lightly coat the cups of a standard non-stick muffin tin with spray.

Lightly mist a small nonstick frying pan with spray and place it over medium heat. Add the onion and bacon and cook for 4 to 6 minutes, or until the onions are just becoming tender. Remove the pan from the heat and set it aside.

Combine the egg whites, milk, mustard, and pepper in a large measuring cup and whisk until well combined. Set aside.

Using a 3¾"-diameter cookie cutter, cut 3 circles out of each tortilla. Microwave them between two paper towels for 15 to 20 seconds, or just long enough for them to become warm and pliable. Then, being careful not to tear the circles, fit each one into a cup in the prepared muffin tin. Next, divide the cheese and the bacon and onion mixture evenly among the cups. Pour the egg mixture into each cup until it is about three-quarters filled. (You may have a small amount leftover.)

Bake the quiches for 20 to 22 minutes, or until the insides are completely set (no longer runny when you insert a butter knife in the center) and the tortillas have taken shape and are lightly crisped on the edges.

Makes 12 quiches

Per serving (3 quiches): **178 calories, 17 g protein, 21 g carbohydrates (3 g sugar), 4 g fat, 1 g saturated fat, 18 mg cholesterol, 2 g fiber, 456 mg sodium**

ROAST BEEF TARTINE

Tartines are a kind of open-faced sandwich popular in France. They're very satisfying and make a terrific lunch—and because they only use one slice of bread instead of two, you'll cut your midday carbs in half.

I make these tartines with any extra-lean roast beef or steak I have on hand—leftover Pittsburgh Steak (page 153), cut as thinly as possible, is an excellent option.

---

1 slice European-style freshly ground whole grain bread (I used Mestemacher Fitness Bread)

2 tablespoons all-natural light, soft spreadable cheese (I used Alouette Garlic & Herbs Soft Spreadable Cheese)

3 ounces all-natural extra-lean, low-sodium roast beef, cut as thinly as possible so it's shaved

¼ cup paper-thin red onion pieces

½ ounce (about 2 tablespoons) thin roasted red bell pepper strips (fresh, not jarred) (see page 36 for roasting instructions)

½ tablespoon drained capers

Place the bread on a cutting board. Spread the cheese evenly over it. Place the roast beef shavings evenly over the cheese. Top that with the onion, peppers, and capers. Cut the tartine in half crosswise. Then cut each half diagonally. Serve immediately.

Makes 1 serving

Per serving: 313 calories, 25 g protein, 30 g carbohydrates (5 g sugar), 11 g fat, 5 g saturated fat, 43 mg cholesterol, 7 g fiber, 585 mg sodium

HARICOTS VERT SALAD WITH GOAT CHEESE

I love the freshness and crunch of this salad. It's essential to "shock" the green beans in an ice bath after you blanch them. This helps them maintain a bright green color and crisp texture. You can use your favorite all-natural, low-fat vinaigrette if you can't find the brand specified below. Any lemon or balsamic-based vinaigrette would complement the flavors nicely.

½ pound trimmed haricots vert (French or baby green beans)

½ cup halved cherry tomatoes

¼ cup red onion slivers

1½ tablespoons all-natural low-fat lemon pesto dressing (I used Simply Boulder Culinary Sauces Lemon Pesto), or your favorite all-natural low-fat vinaigrette

½ ounce goat cheese crumbles

Fill a large soup pot halfway with water and bring it to a boil.

Fill a large bowl halfway with ice water.

Add the beans to the boiling water and cook them for 1 to 3 minutes, or until crisp-tender. Drain, then add them to the bowl with the ice water. When the beans have cooled, remove them from the ice water and pat dry with a paper towel.

Add the beans, tomatoes, and onion to a large glass or plastic bowl. Drizzle with the dressing and toss well to coat. Cover the bowl (or transfer it to a resealable plastic container) and refrigerate for 1 hour. Scoop the salad onto serving plates or a platter. Sprinkle the cheese over top. Serve immediately.

Makes 2 servings

Per serving: 78 calories, 3 g protein, 11 g carbohydrates (5 g sugar), 3 g fat, 1 g saturated fat, 3 mg cholesterol, 5 g fiber, 104 mg sodium

STEAK AU POIVRE WITH CREAM SAUCE

Steak au Poivre literally translates as "pepper steak," and most versions you find at French restaurants have a nice thick crust of black pepper seared onto the outside of the meat. To create the perfect, spicy crust, I put whole peppercorns in a resealable plastic bag and crush them with the flat end of a meat mallet. Don't substitute ground black pepper in this recipe—the meat would taste way too peppery and wouldn't have the right texture.

1 tablespoon + 1 teaspoon coarsely ground or crushed black peppercorns (I used Tellicherry peppercorns)

4 (4-ounce) trimmed bison sirloin steaks, preferably grass fed

Sea salt, to taste

1 teaspoon cornstarch

¼ cup fat-free evaporated milk

Canola oil spray (propellant free)

¼ cup minced shallots

1 teaspoon freshly minced garlic

½ cup all-natural low-sodium beef broth

¼ cup brandy

1 tablespoon all-natural unsalted butter

Press the crushed peppercorns into the steaks to evenly cover them (about 1 teaspoon on each), then sprinkle lightly with salt.

Add the cornstarch to a small bowl. Whisk in just enough milk to form a paste. Then continue whisking in the remaining milk until the mixture is smooth. Set aside.

Place a medium nonstick skillet over medium-high heat. When hot, lightly mist the pan with spray. Add the steaks and cook for 1 minute per side, or until browned on the outsides. Using tongs, stand them on their sides to brown the edges, for 30 seconds to 1 minute longer. Then cook for another minute per side for medium rare, or until desired doneness is reached. Transfer the steaks to a plate and tent them with foil.

Mist the pan again with spray and add the shallots and garlic. Stir for 30 seconds, then add the broth and brandy. Increase the heat to high and let the mixture reduce by about half. Reduce the heat to medium and, whisking constantly, stir in the milk mixture. Cook for 1 to 2 minutes, or until the sauce has thickened slightly. Remove the pan from the heat and stir in the butter until melted. Season with salt and pepper.

Transfer each steak to a serving plate. Divide the sauce evenly among the steaks, about 3 tablespoons on each. Serve immediately.

Makes 4 servings

Per serving: **216 calories, 26 g protein, 6 g carbohydrates (2 g sugar), 6 g fat, 3 g saturated fat, 88 mg cholesterol, <1 g fiber, 98 mg sodium**

Trainer Tip: Brett Hoebel

Go fast, go slow. Interval training—where you exert maximum effort, followed by a period of slowing down and recovery—is a great way to increase your metabolism to burn extra calories and also to strengthen your heart and lungs.

JEN EISENBARTH'S GROUND TURKEY CABBAGE ROLLS

Jen Eisenbarth of Season 3 says, "This is the one cabbage recipe that even non-cabbage-loving people LOVE! Like most moms, I'm always game for a two-for-one deal, so I take any cabbage pieces that are too small [for the cabbage rolls] or are torn, and I cut them, then throw them back into the original pot of water with any and every veggie I have in the fridge. I add a package of fresh chicken breasts and make it into soup. Once the chicken is boiled, I remove the breasts, cut them up, and return them back to the soup. In the time it takes for the cabbage rolls to bake, I have a fresh pot of soup, either for the fridge or freezer!"

Olive oil spray (propellant free)

1 head cabbage

1 cup all-natural canned tomato sauce

1 cup all-natural canned no-salt-added tomato sauce

1 pound extra-lean ground turkey (I used Jennie-O)

1 small onion (about 1 cup), minced

¾ cup cooked parboiled brown rice

¼ teaspoon ground black pepper

¼ cup white vinegar

¼ cup coconut sugar

Preheat the oven to 350°F. Lightly mist a glass or ceramic 13" x 9" baking dish with spray.

Place a large pot (with a tight-fitting lid) of water over high heat. Trim the stem-end of the cabbage head to loosen the core a bit so the leaves will come off the head easier when tender.

When the water is boiling, place the whole cabbage head in the pot, cover, and turn the heat to low. Cook for 8 to 10 minutes, or until the outer leaves are tender. Carefully remove the cabbage from the water and rinse under cold water until it is cool enough to handle. Gently remove the outer leaves, using a knife to slice off the base of the leaves near the core if necessary. (The leaves should remain whole. If they tear, return the cabbage to the boiling water.) Once the leaves are too tough to tear off in one piece, return the cabbage to the water to boil more. Continue removing the cabbage, running it under cold water, and carefully taking outer leaves off, intermittently, until you have 12 whole, large leaves. Drain the leaves well, pat dry, and set aside to cool.

Pour both tomato sauces into a small bowl and mix them well.

In a medium bowl, add the turkey, onion, rice, pepper, and half of the tomato sauce and mix until well combined. Divide into 12 equal portions and shape each into a ball. Place one ball in the center of each

(continued)

cooled cabbage leaf and roll the leaf around it, folding in the sides. Place the cabbage rolls side by side, seam side down, in the prepared baking dish.

Add the vinegar and sugar to the remaining tomato sauce. Stir the mixture until the sugar dissolves. Pour the sauce evenly over the rolls. Cover the dish with foil and bake for 1½ hours, or until the meat is cooked and the cabbage leaves are translucent and very tender.

Makes 4 servings

Per serving (3 rolls): **279 calories, 31 g protein, 37 g carbohydrates (18 g sugar), 2 g fat, trace saturated fat, 45 mg cholesterol, 5 g fiber, 548 mg sodium**

Sarah Nitta

When you're working out and you want to stop . . . don't! Always find opportunities to walk a little extra. Walking should be your very best friend.

GERMAN POTATO SALAD

Traditionally, German potato salad is made with white potatoes. Here I call for light-skinned sweet potatoes, as they are part of The Biggest Loser *food plan, whereas white potatoes are not (see Chapter 2). If you have trouble finding the light-skinned varieties (which tend to be most available during the holiday season), you can substitute red-skinned sweet potatoes.*

Note that it's important to chop your celery and onions before starting to cook, to avoid overcooking your dressing.

1½ pounds peeled light-skinned sweet potatoes, cut in 1" cubes

¼ teaspoon + ⅛ teaspoon sea salt, plus more to taste, if desired

2 teaspoons whole wheat pastry flour

¼ cup apple cider vinegar

3 tablespoons water

1½ teaspoons all-natural Dijon mustard

2 tablespoons coconut sugar

2 ounces (about 2 slices) lean, nitrate-free smoked turkey bacon (I used Applegate Hardwood Smoked Uncured Turkey Bacon), cut into ¼" pieces

⅓ cup finely chopped onion

¼ cup diced celery

¼ cup finely chopped fresh parsley

⅛ teaspoon ground black pepper, or to taste

Place the potatoes in a large nonstick soup pot. Cover them by at least 1" with cold water and add ¼ teaspoon salt. Place the pan over high heat and bring the water to a boil. Boil the potatoes for 6 to 9 minutes, or until fork-tender. Drain and transfer the potatoes to a medium bowl.

Spoon the flour into a small bowl or measuring cup. Whisk in enough vinegar to form a paste. Whisk in the remaining vinegar and water until no lumps remain. Then whisk in the mustard and sugar until well combined. Set the dressing aside.

Place a small nonstick skillet over medium-high heat. Add the bacon and cook for 3 to 5 minutes, or until it starts to crisp. Remove from the heat and add to the potatoes.

Place the skillet back on the heat. Add the reserved dressing and boil, stirring frequently with a wooden spoon, for 1 minute, or until it's as thick as gravy. Remove from the heat.

Add the onion, celery, and parsley to the potatoes. Add the dressing and mix until well combined. Season with the pepper and the ⅛ teaspoon salt. Serve warm or chilled.

Makes 6 (generous ½-cup) servings

Per serving: 128 calories, 4 g protein, 27 g carbohydrates (10 g sugar), less than 1 g fat, trace saturated fat, 8 mg cholesterol, 4 g fiber, 273 mg sodium

PLACKI KARTOFLANE (POLISH POTATO PANCAKES)

I prefer to use light-skinned sweet potatoes over the red-skinned ones for these pancakes. Though you can add the toppings suggested below, I like them best with just an extra touch of sea salt. Sour cream and applesauce are traditional accompaniments to potato pancakes, but be mindful that each tablespoon of all-natural low-fat sour cream (depending on the brand) has about 35 to 40 calories and 2 to 3 grams of fat. All-natural unsweetened applesauce has about 12 to 15 calories per ¼ cup.

1½ pounds light-skinned sweet potatoes, peeled and cut into 1½" cubes

Olive oil spray (propellant free)

¼ cup + 2 tablespoons all-natural egg substitute

½ cup grated sweet onion

¼ teaspoon salt, plus more to taste

1½ tablespoons whole grain oat flour, or more, if necessary

All-natural low-fat sour cream or all-natural unsweetened applesauce (optional)

Fill a large saucepan about half-full with water and place it over high heat. When the water comes to a boil, add the potatoes. Cook for 3 minutes, or until the potatoes are somewhat hard in the middle but starting to soften on the outside. Drain and rinse with cold water. Set aside until cool enough to handle.

Preheat the oven to 450°F. Line 2 large baking sheets (or work in batches if you only have 1) with nonstick aluminum foil. Lightly mist the foil with spray.

Add half of the well-drained potatoes to the bowl of a large food processor fitted with a chopping blade. Pulse intermittently, stopping to scrape the sides of the bowl, until they are chopped (see note). Transfer the potatoes to a large glass or plastic bowl. Repeat with the remaining potatoes. Once all the potatoes are in the bowl, stir in the egg substitute, onion, and salt until well combined. Add the flour, ½ tablespoon at a time, until the potato mixture sticks together slightly and is not too wet.

Divide the mixture into 12 relatively equal portions and place 6 on each baking sheet, evenly spaced. Press each portion into a 4" pancake, making sure they do not touch.

Lightly mist the tops of the pancakes with spray. Place the baking sheets side by side in the oven (not one on top of the other, or they will not brown evenly). Bake for 15 minutes. Gently flip the pancakes,

(continued)

mist the tops with spray, and bake for 10 to 13 minutes longer, or until crisp and lightly browned (bake longer for crisper edges).

Divide the pancakes among 4 serving plates. Season with additional salt or top with sour cream or applesauce, if desired. Serve immediately.

Makes 12 pancakes

Note: *Most of the potatoes should be finely chopped, but be sure not to chop them so much that they become mushy.*

Per serving (3 pancakes): **144 calories, 5 g protein, 30 g carbohydrates (9 g sugar), trace fat, trace saturated fat, 0 mg cholesterol, 5 g fiber, 273 mg sodium**

Irene Alvarado

Keep moving and don't stop! If you work out in the morning, you'll burn more calories throughout the day. Then you can go to bed at a decent time and get plenty of rest.

KIELBASA (POLISH SMOKED SAUSAGE)

You will need either a wood roasting plank (that you can place in your oven) or a grill plank for your barbecue grill to smoke these sausages. The wood roasting plank is a little more expensive (in the short run only) than the throw-away planks for the grill. I got mine at Sur La Table, but both are available at various online sites.

1 pound extra-lean ground pork

1 tablespoon paprika

2 teaspoons freshly minced garlic

¾ teaspoon kosher salt

½ teaspoon all-natural liquid smoke (I used Wright's All-Natural Hickory Seasoning Liquid Smoke)

½ teaspoon freshly ground black pepper

Place a sheet of waxed paper or parchment on a clean, flat work surface. Preheat the grill to high or the oven to the temperature as directed on the plank instructions.

Add the pork, paprika, garlic, salt, liquid smoke, and pepper to a medium bowl. Using your hands, mix for 2 minutes, making sure that the meat and seasonings are well incorporated. Divide the mixture into 8 equal portions. Shape each into a log that is 4" long and an even thickness.

Follow the package directions for your grill or oven plank (most grill planks require soaking prior to grilling; most oven planks need to be warmed in the oven prior to adding the food). Place the logs on the plank in a single layer so they do not touch. Roast or grill them according to the plank instructions, or until no longer pink inside (mine were perfectly cooked in my oven after 18 to 20 minutes at 350°F).

Makes 4 servings

Per serving (2 sausages): 151 calories, 26 g protein, 2 g carbohydrates (trace sugar), 4 g fat, 1 g saturated fat, 75 mg cholesterol, <1 g fiber, 494 mg sodium

International Desserts

As anyone who owns a cookbook by Chef Devin knows, she takes her desserts *very* seriously. "I respect my desserts," she says. "When I eat them, it's supposed to be an indulgence. Dessert should be satisfying and decadent. It should taste like something you're not supposed to eat."

As someone who has maintained an impressive 70-pound weight loss for years, Devin acknowledged that for a long time she "white-knuckled it" when it came to sweets—she just couldn't let herself have desserts, for fear that one small taste could turn into a full-on binge. But in recent years, she says she's developed a balanced approach to enjoying sweets without overindulging. "I don't even like to set aside one treat day," she said. "Instead of really indulging big on one day, I prefer to have just a little treat every day."

One of the best ways to keep sweet cravings in check is to be sure to eat enough calories throughout the day and to eat meals and snacks at consistent intervals. If you feel full and satisfied, you're less likely to want something sweet. Bit if you're hungry and your blood sugar has plummeted, you're likely to reach for a doughnut before you even realize what you're doing.

When you do have dessert, Devin's "a little treat every day" approach makes perfect sense. You'll enjoy your dessert more when you don't have to feel guilty about eating it. And don't forget to eat mindfully and slowly.

Devin said she's especially excited about the Tiramisu Custard (page 194) that she and her team came up with. While it's not a traditional tiramisu, she says, "The flavor is extremely similar. They're just perfect!" And at just 101 calories, it's an everyday indulgence you can enjoy any day of the week. Hope you saved room for dessert!

CHOCOLATE RASPBERRY CREPES

Sweet and savory crepes are eaten throughout France. Sometimes they're filled with meat or cheese for breakfast or lunch, other times they're slathered with chocolate and fresh fruit. I love the taste of chocolate and raspberries together, and this recipe will feel indulgent at only 145 calories per crepe!

Note that you may have a little leftover batter. Be sure to use a full 2 tablespoons for each crepe. If you use less, you may have trouble getting the batter to cover the bottom of the pan, which will make it difficult to create uniformly circle crepes.

3¼ cups raspberries, plus additional for garnish, if desired, divided

1¼ cups all-natural fat-free ricotta cheese

1 tablespoon + ¼ cup light agave nectar, divided

⅓ cup whole grain oat flour

4 tablespoons unsweetened cocoa powder, divided

2 tablespoons coconut sugar

Pinch salt

6 large egg whites

2 tablespoons unsweetened plain almond milk

2 tablespoons fat-free evaporated milk

2 tablespoons melted all-natural butter alternative (I used Earth Balance Original Organic Buttery Spread)

Canola oil spray (propellant free)

Add 1¼ cups of the raspberries, the ricotta, and 1 tablespoon agave to the bowl of a food processor fitted with a chopping blade. Process until relatively smooth, stopping to scrape down the bowl intermittently, if needed. Transfer the mixture to a resealable plastic container and refrigerate until ready to fill the crepes.

In a small mixing bowl, stir together the flour, 2 tablespoons of the cocoa powder, the sugar, and salt. In another small bowl, whisk together the egg whites, almond milk, and evaporated milk until well combined. Whisking constantly, add the melted butter until well combined. Whisk in the flour mixture just until no lumps remain (it may separate slightly, which is okay). Let the batter stand 10 minutes.

In another small bowl, use a spoon to mix ¼ cup agave with the remaining 2 tablespoons cocoa powder.

Place an 8" or 9" nonstick skillet over medium heat (see note). When the pan is warm, lift it off the heat and mist it with spray. Immediately add 2 slightly heaping tablespoons of the crepe batter and twist your wrist to swirl the batter so it spreads to the edges of the pan. Replace it on the heat and let it cook for 30 seconds to 1 minute, or until lightly set. Carefully, using a large spatula, flip it and let it cook for 30 seconds to 1 minute longer, or until cooked through. Transfer it to a dinner plate. Repeat with the remaining batter, misting the pan with spray between each crepe. If you find your pan is getting too hot (and the batter cooks before you have a chance to swirl it to the edges),

(continued)

reduce the heat or remove it from the heat momentarily (if it's too hot, swirling the batter out to the edges of the pan will be nearly impossible).

Place one crepe on a plate so the lighter side is face up. Spoon about ¼ cup of the refrigerated filling in a 2"-wide strip down the center of the crepe. Top it evenly with ¼ cup raspberries. Roll the outside to cover the filling, then gently flip the filled crepe so the seam faces down. Drizzle about ½ tablespoon of the cocoa-agave mixture evenly over the top. Repeat with the remaining crepes, filling, and topping. Garnish with additional raspberries, if desired.

Makes 8 crepes

Note: *It's very important that you use a good nonstick pan for this recipe, or else the crepes could stick and rip.*

Per crepe: 145 calories, 7 g protein, 25 g carbohydrates (15 g sugar), 3 g fat, <1 g saturated fat, 0 mg cholesterol, 5 g fiber, 103 mg sodium

Trainer Tip: Bob Harper

A "treat day" every so often is fine, if you've been eating clean the other 6 days of the week. You can go out with your friends and have a slice of pizza as long as you get back on track the next day.

RASPBERRY SOUFFLÉS

If you really want to impress your guests with an elegant, French-inspired dinner, serve them Steak au Poivre (page 178) as the entrée and these soufflés for dessert. Though they look very impressive when they first come out of the oven, I think they taste even better the next day (though they will deflate as they sit). These feel like an indulgence, but they are so low in calories, you don't have to reserve this dessert for special occasions.

Butter-flavored cooking spray

⅔ cup fresh raspberries

¼ cup coconut sugar

1 tablespoon raspberry liqueur

3 large egg whites

⅛ teaspoon cream of tartar

Preheat the oven to 350°F. Lightly mist five 3½"-diameter (½-cup capacity) ramekins with spray.

In the bowl of a mini food processor fitted with a chopping blade or a blender, process the raspberries, pausing to scrape down the sides of the bowl if necessary, until they are completely smooth. Place a fine mesh strainer over a medium mixing bowl. Pour the raspberry puree into the strainer and, using a spatula, press it through the strainer. Discard the seeds. Stir in the sugar and liqueur until well combined. Set aside.

Add the egg whites and cream of tartar to a clean, dry, medium metal or glass mixing bowl. Using a hand or stand mixer fitted with the whisk attachment, beat the whites until they are stiff but not dry. Using a spatula, gently fold them in three additions into the raspberry puree, being careful not to overmix them.

Divide the mixture evenly among the prepared ramekins. Bake for 7 to 10 minutes, or until the soufflés have poofed well above the dish and are golden brown on top and no longer runny inside when poked in the center with a butter knife. Serve immediately.

Makes 5 soufflés

Per soufflé: 63 calories, 2 g protein, 13 g carbohydrates (8 g sugar), trace fat, trace saturated fat, 0 mg cholesterol, 1 g fiber, 55 mg sodium

TIRAMISU CUSTARD

Tiramisu is the quintessential Italian dessert—but it's also one of the heaviest, most calorie-laden desserts you'll find on any restaurant menu. I'd given it up years ago after losing weight, but this custard does insanely well to mimic the flavors without leaving anything on your hips. Just remember to shake your can of evaporated milk before pouring it since, since as it sits, the milk separates.

1 large omega-3 egg

2 tablespoons Marsala wine

1 packet (0.25 ounce) unflavored gelatin

1 teaspoon instant espresso powder

1 cup boiling water

½ cup cold fat-free evaporated milk

½ cup all-natural, low-fat ricotta cheese

⅓ cup coconut sugar

1 teaspoon unsweetened cocoa powder

In the jar of a blender, blend the egg, wine, gelatin, and espresso powder on high for 15 seconds. Turn off the blender and, using a rubber spatula, scrape down the sides, then blend the ingredients for another 10 seconds. Let the mixture stand for a minute. Add the boiling water and immediately blend for 15 seconds, or until the gelatin is dissolved. Add the milk, ricotta, and sugar and continue blending for 1 minute, or until the mixture is smooth.

Divide the mixture evenly among six 3½"-diameter (½-cup capacity) ramekins or decorative custard dishes. Cover each with plastic wrap and refrigerate for at least 3 hours, or until set. Dust the tops evenly with the cocoa powder. Serve immediately.

Makes 6 servings

Per serving: **101 calories, 6 g protein, 15 g carbohydrates (12 g sugar), 2 g fat, <1 g saturated fat, 43 mg cholesterol, trace fiber, 114 mg sodium**

BLUEBERRY CRUMBLE

Blueberry crumble is consumed all across the United States, of course, but Southerners (and Mainers!) are true blueberry crumble connoisseurs. I wish I could tell you that you could substitute frozen blueberries for fresh in this recipe, but the truth is, they just don't work. I know frozen berries can be more convenient, but fresh berries are essential to make this crumble as delicious as it can be.

Canola oil spray (propellant free)

¼ cup whole grain oat flour

34 ounces (about 8 cups) fresh blueberries

¼ cup + 2 tablespoons light agave nectar

2 tablespoons freshly squeezed lemon juice

1 cup old-fashioned oats

2 tablespoons very cold unsalted butter, cut into cubes

1 tablespoon 100% fruit blueberry or mixed berry spread

Preheat the oven to 350°F. Light mist an 8" x 8" glass or ceramic baking dish with spray.

Add the flour to the bowl of a mini food processor fitted with a chopping blade. Process it for 2 minutes.

In a medium mixing bowl, mix the blueberries, agave, lemon juice, and flour until well combined. Transfer the mixture to the prepared baking dish. Set aside.

In a small mixing bowl, combine the oats, butter, and fruit spread using a pastry blender until well combined. Sprinkle the oat mixture evenly over the fruit mixture.

Bake for 45 to 50 minutes, or until the berries are tender and hot throughout (only some juices should remain in the bottom of the pan; it shouldn't be runny), and the topping is golden brown. Transfer the dish to a wire rack and cool for 10 to 15 minutes. Cut into 6 pieces. Serve immediately.

Makes 6 servings

Per serving: **251 calories, 4 g protein, 49 g carbohydrates (32 g sugar), 6 g fat, 2 g saturated fat, 10 mg cholesterol, 6 g fiber, 2 mg sodium**

THAI FRUIT SALAD

Lychee (or litchi) is often added to this salad in Thai restaurants. If you can find fresh lychee fruit, feel free to add it. Each lychee (depending on size) adds only about 3 to 10 total calories. But be sure to check labels if you opt for canned lychee. They're often filled with sugars or preservatives.

To cube a papaya, simply peel the fruit using a knife or veggie peeler, then cut it in half lengthwise. Scoop out the seeds with a spoon and discard them. You're now ready to cube the flesh.

---

3 cups fresh pineapple cubes (about half of 1 medium pineapple)

2 cups fresh papaya cubes (about 1 medium papaya)

2 cups orange sections (about 3 medium oranges), all peel and membranes removed

Zest of 1 lime (about 1½ tablespoons), plus additional to garnish, if desired

3 tablespoons freshly squeezed lime juice

2 tablespoons coconut sugar

2 firm medium bananas (about 2 cups), cut into bite-size rounds

In a large resealable plastic container, combine the pineapple, papaya, orange sections, and lime zest.

In a small bowl, mix the lime juice and sugar until the sugar is mostly dissolved. Pour the liquid over the fruit and toss until well combined. Cover and refrigerate for at least 30 minutes for the flavors to meld.

Just before serving, add the bananas (this will keep them from getting mushy) and toss the fruit salad. Serve in pineapple shells (mini or full-size), papaya shells, or martini glasses. Top with additional lime zest, if desired.

Makes 8 (heaping ¾-cup) servings

Per serving: **105 calories, 1 g protein, 27 g carbohydrates (20 g sugar), trace fat, trace saturated fat, 0 mg cholesterol, 4 g fiber, 9 mg sodium**

Don Evans

Pay attention to everything you eat. It all boils down to calories in versus calories out. Do the math.

JAPANESE TART GREEN TEA FROZEN YOGURT

It's tough to go to a Japanese restaurant without being faced with the option of ordering green tea . . . heck, sometimes it's even served for free at the end of a meal. This cool, creamy take on the traditional hot tea will give you all the satisfaction of a dessert, combining the unique flavor of green tea with the distinctive tartness of frozen yogurt.

Be sure to buy pure matcha powder for this recipe, not "sweet" matcha. I've found that various brands of matcha powder vary widely. Some yield a stronger flavor than others, so feel free to use less or more as desired.

2 tablespoons light agave nectar

1 tablespoon vanilla

1½ teaspoons all-natural unsweetened matcha (green tea) powder (page xiv)

2 teaspoons stevia

2 cups all-natural fat-free Greek yogurt (I used Fage)

In a medium mixing bowl, whisk together the agave, vanilla, matcha powder, and stevia until well combined and no lumps remain. Stir in the yogurt until well combined. If there are visible green flecks (the matcha powder), using a spatula, push them along the side of the bowl to break them up as you continue stirring.

Spoon the mixture into the bowl of an ice cream maker that is at least 2 quarts. Make the frozen yogurt according to the manufacturer's directions. Serve immediately or freeze for harder consistency.

Makes 4 (½-cup) servings

Per serving: **107 calories, 11 g protein, 14 g carbohydrates (25 g sugar), 0 g fat, 0 g saturated fat, 0 mg cholesterol, 0 fiber, 48 mg sodium**

Jay Jacobs

I really can eat much healthier than I ever would have thought, and my sugar cravings are gone. I feel confident that I can take what I am learning every day at the Ranch and make it my new lifestyle.

MEXICAN HOT CHOCOLATE

Mexican hot chocolate is a spicier version of this classic winter drink and often contains a kick of chili powder in addition to sweet spices like cinnamon. Feel free to adjust the seasoning to your preference. This hot chocolate is very rich, so it will do well to satisfy your chocolate craving, provide comfort, and keep you from needing to do an extra-long workout to burn off dessert—the ideal combination!

1 tablespoon agave nectar

2 tablespoons all-natural unsweetened cocoa powder with at least 2 grams of fiber per tablespoon (I used Wonderslim Wondercocoa)

2 tablespoons fat-free evaporated milk

¾ cup unsweetened plain almond milk

Pinch ground cinnamon, or more to taste

Pinch chili powder (optional)

In a 1-cup glass measuring cup or medium bowl, whisk together the agave, cocoa powder, and evaporated milk until no lumps remain. Whisk in the almond milk. If any of the chocolate mixture remains in the bottom of the cup, use a spatula to incorporate it.

Transfer the mixture to a small saucepan and place over medium heat. Continue stirring until hot. Stir in the cinnamon and chili powder, if desired. Pour into a mug and serve immediately.

Makes 1 serving

Per serving: 155 calories, 5 g protein, 28 g carbohydrates (20 g sugar), 2 g fat, 0 saturated fat, 0 mg cholesterol, 5 g fiber, 175 mg sodium

Trainer Tip: Cara Castronuova

Healthy snacking is a good thing! It will help prevent you from overeating at meals by curbing hunger.

Essentials

What you may have thought of in the past as "essentials" for your kitchen—flour, sugar, butter, salt, bread—have now likely been replaced by a new set of must-haves, such as fresh fruits and vegetables, grilled chicken and fish, egg whites, nuts, and whole grains. Keeping your pantry and fridge stocked with these essentials is the difference between falling off the wagon and going to sleep at night knowing you had a day of healthy eating within your calorie budget. In the famous words of trainer Jillian Michaels, "If you fail to plan, you plan to fail."

As Chef Devin attests, even a professional chef has to prepare for healthy eating at home. "When I get home from work, I'm exhausted," says Devin. "That's the time when I most don't feel like cooking. So having essentials on hand in my fridge means I don't have the option of making a bad choice. I can throw together a simple meal with minimal effort, and I know it's going to be healthy."

Stocking essentials like fruit and nuts (in preportioned baggies) is also a perfect solution for in-between-meal snacking. That stretch between lunch and dinner can be a tempting time, but when you have your go-to snacks at your fingertips, you're less likely to run to the coffee shop for a jumbo-size muffin.

As *The Biggest Loser* contestants discover each season, it's important to give your body what it needs so that you can get on with the work of burning calories. As Season 6's Jerry Skeabeck says, "Food is definitely fuel for the body. The right type of fuel must go into it to make it work efficiently. Preplan your day's calories, because in this fast-paced world, you often have to make quick decisions about what to eat. Remember your goal and choose wisely."

Good advice from a pro who knows just how important it is to have a strategy for eating healthy. The recipes in this chapter will show you how to create the essentials you'll need to whip up many of the healthy dishes in this book—or to improvise and create your own new favorites. When you have these basic staples on hand, your options are limitless.

Trainer Tip: Bob Harper

What makes *Biggest Losers* winners? It's their driving force on a daily basis. No matter what they're feeling, whatever is obstructing them, they'll do anything it takes to win. They have a winner's mentality. You can apply that same attitude to your weight-loss journey!

ESSENTIAL GRILLED CHICKEN

Any good cookbook author knows not to repeat recipes from one book to the next. That said, it is virtually impossible for me to write a healthy cookbook without including a recipe for basic grilled chicken, an essential item for controlling weight. I recommend keeping extra grilled chicken on hand at all times to toss into salads, layer into sandwiches, and sprinkle on pizzas and quesadillas for a healthy protein punch.

4 (4-ounce) trimmed boneless, skinless chicken breasts

Olive oil spray (propellant free)

Salt, to taste

Ground black pepper, to taste

Preheat a grill to high heat.

Lightly mist both sides of each chicken breast with spray and sprinkle lightly with salt and pepper. Grill for 3 to 5 minutes per side, or until no longer pink. Serve immediately.

Makes 4 servings

Per serving: 127 calories, 26 g protein, 0 g carbohydrates (0 g sugar), 2 g fat, trace saturated fat, 66 mg cholesterol, 0 g fiber, 74 mg sodium

Olivia Ward

Get up and get moving! You don't need a fancy gym to burn calories. You can walk around your office, walk outside, park your car far from the nearest entrance at the mall, or walk around your couch as you watch TV at night. You will be surprised at how many calories you will burn throughout the day!

HOMEMADE CHORIZO

This sausage can be used in many different ways. You can shape it into links or patties, or crumble it. Trust me, you'll enjoy it—and your body will enjoy it much more than eating the traditional version, which is often made from some of the fattiest (not to mention least appealing) parts of the pig and can contain upwards of 28 grams of fat!

¼ cup + 1 tablespoon old-fashioned oats

¼ cup red wine vinegar

2 tablespoons all-natural egg substitute

¼ cup chili powder

2 teaspoons freshly minced garlic

1 teaspoon dried oregano

½ teaspoon salt

1 pound extra-lean ground pork

Combine the oats, vinegar, and egg substitute in a medium bowl. Allow to stand for 3 minutes, or until the oats begin to soften. Add the chili powder, garlic, oregano, and salt and stir until well combined. Using your clean hands or a fork, mix in the pork until well combined. Transfer the mixture to a resealable plastic container and refrigerate at least 24 hours before using.

Makes 8 (2-ounce) servings

Per serving: **101 calories, 14 g protein, 5 g carbohydrates (trace sugar), 3 g fat, <1 g saturated fat, 37 mg cholesterol, 2 g fiber, 221 mg sodium**

Deni Hill

Find a form of exercise you enjoy. If you have fun, you'll be more likely to do it.

ASIAN PEANUT SAUCE

This is one of my favorite go-to sauces, and I use it in many of my Asian recipes. It contains much less fat and sugar than any bottled version I've been able to find in the supermarket, and it adds a real richness to a variety of Asian dishes.

1 tablespoon all-natural lower-sodium soy sauce

2 teaspoons coconut sugar

½ teaspoon chili-infused extra-virgin olive oil

½ teaspoon salt-free Szechwan seasoning (I used The Spice Hunter Salt Free Szechwan Seasoning Blend)

1½ tablespoons all-natural creamy peanut butter

1 tablespoon rice vinegar

In a small bowl, mix the soy sauce and sugar. Add the oil and seasoning and mix until combined. Whisk in the peanut butter until smooth. Whisk in the vinegar until smooth. Add immediately to your favorite dish or refrigerate it in a resealable container for up to 5 days.

Makes ¼ cup

Per serving (2 tablespoons): **109 calories, 3 g protein, 8 g carbohydrates (4 g sugar), 7 g fat, 1 g saturated fat, 0 cholesterol, 1 g fiber, 256 mg sodium**

BROCCOLI PESTO

I love the flavor of pesto, but most bottled pesto sauces are full of fat and calories. This lighter version combines the traditional flavors of garlic and basil, but uses Greek yogurt and broccoli to create a lighter, fresher-tasting finished product. Make sure your steamed broccoli is well drained before you process it; otherwise, it can water down the pesto.

2 cups (about 7 ounces) steamed broccoli florets, cooled to at least room temperature

16 large basil leaves (about ⅓ cup packed)

4 medium cloves garlic, roughly chopped

2 tablespoons freshly grated all-natural Parmesan cheese

2 tablespoons all-natural low-sodium vegetable broth

2 teaspoons extra-virgin olive oil

1 cup all-natural fat-free plain Greek yogurt

¾ teaspoon sea salt

Ground black pepper, to taste

Add the broccoli, basil, garlic, and Parmesan to the bowl of a food processor fitted with a chopping blade. Pulse several times, until the ingredients are finely chopped. Making sure the food processor is turned off, scrape down the bowl and add the broth and oil. Process until the mixture is finely chopped and somewhat smooth (it should resemble a traditional basil pesto).

Spoon the mixture into a medium glass or plastic bowl. Add the yogurt and salt and stir until well combined. Season with pepper. Use immediately or store in an airtight plastic container for up to 2 days.

Makes 2 cups

Per serving (about ¼ cup): 46 calories, 5 g protein, 4 g carbohydrates (<1 g sugar), 2 g fat, trace saturated fat, 1 mg cholesterol, 1 g fiber, 184 mg sodium

FISH TACO SAUCE

Fish tacos are often served with a heavy, lemony mayonnaise sauce. Though I have found one or two light versions of lemon mayonnaise on the market, they either are not light enough for my taste or are full of artificial ingredients. Here's a quick throw-together version that's just as delicious and adds that essential creamy texture to fish tacos.

½ cup all-natural light mayonnaise (I used Spectrum Light Canola Mayo)

4 packets (0.8 gram each) crystallized lemon (I used True Lemon)

2 teaspoons fat-free milk

½ teaspoon garlic powder

½ teaspoon paprika

2 pinches ground red pepper

In a small resealable plastic container, whisk together the mayonnaise, lemon, milk, garlic powder, paprika, and red pepper until well combined. Serve immediately, or cover and refrigerate for up to 3 days.

Makes a heaping ½ cup

Per serving (1 tablespoon): 32 calories, trace protein, trace carbohydrates (trace sugar), 3 g fat, 0 g saturated fat, trace cholesterol, 99 mg sodium

Trainer Tip: Bob Harper

Growing up, I knew that I would always have to look out for myself. I could beat myself up or be my own best friend. And I chose to be my own best friend. You have got to have yourself in your corner.

Acknowledgments

Devin Alexander

I am so insanely grateful to be a consistent part of *The Biggest Loser* family. Not only do I get to play a tiny role in helping change lives daily, but I also have the ultimate privilege of working with some of the most amazing professionals in the business!

The whole team at Rodale rocks . . . particularly: Julie Will who happens to be a brilliant editor *and* who knows the value (and necessity!) of guilty pleasures as a part of succeeding with a long-term healthy lifestyle; production editor superhero Nancy N. Bailey, who makes sure the trains run on time; designer Christina Gaugler who made the pages look so enticing with the help of killer photographers, Mitch Mandel and Tom McDonald; the oh-so-talented and sweet Melissa Roberson, who brings Southern hospitality to everything she does and who spent hours writing the nonrecipe portions of the book; publisher extraordinaire Karen Rinaldi; publicity goddesses Emily Weber and Yelena Nesbit; and Robin Shallow, who has supported me for years and might possibly be the "Real-life Wonder Woman." Really. I mean it. I think she is! I've said it before and I'll say it again!!!

Thanks to Dr. Michael Dansinger, who is extremely professional and knowledgeable beyond words *and* who makes my job so much easier in his ability to realize that there has to be some flexibility in our diets.

To the ultimate coordinator, Edwin Karapetian. And to Reveille's Vice President of Brand Development and Production, Chad Bennett, who's worked with me on every book and whom I just absolutely adore beyond words.

To the producers and executives of *The Biggest Loser,* particularly Howard Owens of Reveille and Todd Nelson and J. D. Roth of 3 Ball Productions, who made me the happiest girl ever when they first invited me into *The Biggest Loser* family. To Kim Niemi, Neysa Siefert, and Joni Camacho from NBC Universal and to Dave Broome and Yong Yam from 25/7 Productions, who are simply the best!

To Jillian Michaels and Bob Harper for embracing me and my work. To all *The Biggest Loser* contestants who've spent time in my kitchen and let me spend time in theirs, inspiring so many of my creations. To Chef Cameron Payne and Renee Jarvis of *The Biggest Loser* Resort, where everyone should absolutely visit!

To Robert Schueller and Melissa, herself, of Melissa's Produce who supplied us with our out-of-season produce when no grocery stores carried it. To Sara Wing and the team at Cabot's who provided plenty of their insanely great 75 percent reduced-fat cheddar cheese. To Christine Dooley and the team at Sargento who supplied the best light provolone and Swiss ever! To the team at Eden foods who stock more natural, healthy products than almost any other company, from no-salt-added black beans to 100 percent whole grain Udon noodles to the best-ever hot sesame oil. To Seth Mendelsohn and Simply Boulder for shipping their yummy dressings. And to Joe Collerd of the Spice Hunter who donated more varieties of their salt-free seasonings than I even realized existed until I started writing this book, instantly changing my world!!!

To Test Kitchen Goddess Stephanie Farrell; Go-to-Gal Michele Canatella; Alexandra Gudmundsson, who has been unofficially deemed Chef Speedy; Angela Nehmens and Jennifer Nettleton who made every day in my kitchen a blast while lending their incredible expertise! To my mother, Toni Simone, who when I hurt my back and thought I might miss a book deadline for the first time ever, flew across the country to rescue the book . . . and me—I am eternally grateful for the weeks I got to spend with her and for all of her hard work!

And a very special thanks to publicists Carrie Simons, Ashley Sandberg, and Jim Eber, whose advice and guidance is irreplaceable! And to Rock Star James Emley, whose support (and grocery runs for me) made it possible to complete the book and whose massage skills kept a smile on my face even when I couldn't quite move. Oip! Oip!

Melissa Roberson

The Biggest Loser is a family and a community, and I'm honored to be part of it. Thanks as always to each and every cast member who shares their stories with me—their ups, their downs, their setbacks, their achievements. It feeds me every day. Working with you is the best part of my job.

Also thanks to the larger *Biggest Loser* family including Cheryl Forberg, RD, nutritionist for the show, and Chad Bennett, who has worked magic for me, lo, these many seasons. And Bob Harper, always love sharing a laugh and an audio blog with you.

Thanks also to Devin for your help and hospitality—working with you is always a treat (metaphorically and literally—when I'm at your house!)

To Julie Will, my book editor: My trust and faith in you will never flag.

And to my own family, human and feline, for purrs and support: Sal, Chet, and Kitty Carlisle.

Index

Underscored page references indicate sidebars. **Boldface** references indicate photographs and illustrations.